# From Fear to Love:
## My Private Journey

By

Donna Lynn

Library of Congress Cataloging-in-Publication Data

Lynn, Donna – 1957 -

*From Fear to Love: My Private Journey* by Donna Lynn

A story of lifelong interaction with beings from another world.

1. UFOs  2. Abductions  3. Extraterrestrials  4. Metaphysical

I. Donna Lynn, 1957- II. UFOs III. Metaphysical IV. Title

Library of Congress Catalog Card Number: 2017930958
ISBN: 9781940265407

Cover Art and Layout: www.vril8.com
Book set in: Minion Pro, Viner Hand ITC
Book Design: Tab Pillar
Published by:

PO Box 754, Huntsville, AR 72740
800-935-0045 or 479-738-2348; fax 479-738-2448
WWW.OZARKMT.COM
Printed in the United States of America

# Table of Contents

# Introduction

This is my attempt to describe the indescribable, comprehend the incomprehensible, and explain the unexplainable. It's the story of my private journey from Fear to Love with the assistance of alien lifeforms; the journey from running away to gradually finding acceptance and then embracing that which used to terrify me. I have documented my mystic travels from the murky dark swirling waters of Fear, up the treacherous waterfall against the current of Insecurity into the crystalline warm embrace of the clear sea of Love.

This information doesn't fit into a typical beginning, middle, and end format. The aliens work in a circular and spiraling motion. They are not linear and their interactions with us don't match up into tidy cubbyholes. Our relationship is more like a dance in the chaos; a dance to a song without a melody or a rhythm I can recognize, played on musical instruments that I've never seen. Thus I have done my best to put together forty-plus years' worth of notes and make sense of it, grouping in categories rather than by timeline. The text in italics is directly taken from my journals. Some years I was very good at journaling and tracking dates, dreams, impressions, and visions; other times I was not. The visitations come and go in cycles, and if they coincided with a stressful period of my life I was not very meticulous with record-keeping. I keep journals in a bedside drawer and grab one and begin writing after an encounter; thus each journal contains entries and sketches from different years, different phases of connection and communication. The aliens encouraged me to remember specific things that are of utmost importance, and if I didn't write them down they would repeat the message until I did, so I am hopeful that I have included the most vital information. The bold text is verbatim from the aliens. As I became less terrified, more interested and curious, it became easier to hear and understand their messages in their own words.

The dark heavy secret I have carried is that a deep and important portion of my life involves interaction and friendships with beings that are alien. It is now time to bring this secret out from the darkest recesses of my memories and shine a spotlight upon it, so that others—and I know there are many—need not feel alone or frightened any longer, and those who are curious and desire to be a part of this may do so. We are at an important crossroads for humanity and the Earth, and my fervent wish is that that Love will win out over Fear—but at present, the final result remains to be seen.

# Chapter 1

## Fear

I'm naked and afraid. As soon as I am consciously aware of my nakedness I cross my arms over my breasts, tucking my legs underneath me so as not to be sitting squarely on the cold floor. I am mildly dazed and unsure where I am. The walls and floor are stark white; the air is chilly and smells odd, sour, like fermented vegetables. The room is round with a flat floor; no door, no windows. Probably sixty or seventy people stand and sit with backs against the circular wall, consciously avoiding eye contact with one another. A few of us are naked; others wear pajamas or nightgowns or robes; some are fully dressed in their day clothes. One lady has large pink curlers in her hair. Another wears a sparkly silver evening gown with long gloves and high heels as she leans against the white wall, her glamorous makeup smeared with tears as she sobs quietly. A girl about twelve, wearing a pink flannel nightgown, snuggles on the floor with her cat. We try to remain still and silent though a few quiet murmurs, moans, and sighs can be heard echoing, bouncing across the round walls. We are old and young; black, brown, and white; male and female. We are samples of humanity from around the globe. It's the children I feel sorry for, but know from past encounters that I can do nothing to help them or myself. I try to smile at a young black girl, and her glassy stare reveals nothing but utter terror. We've all been here before. Yes, even the children.

A door glides open, appearing from the nothingness in the wall. People gasp, muttering incoherently, and those standing close to it scatter quickly away like cockroaches. My arms tighten around my chest, holding myself, trying to feel reassured and safe. But I am neither reassured nor safe, and I know it.

Three beings glide through the doorway and come to hover in the middle of the room, looking around with huge unblinking eyes, observing us, taking mental notes. One of them stares directly at me. It is small, about the size of a six-year-old child. It has a head that is disproportionately large for its tiny, skinny body. I can't tell if it is wearing clothes or not. *Why does it matter if we are clothed?* I hear a booming voice, belying the size of the being, inside my head as it stares at me with large piercing glistening black eyes. *It matters not that you are undressed.* My own nakedness went far deeper than bare breasts; it tore its way down to my very soul. This being knew my thoughts, knew my feelings, knew my fears by way of those eyes boring through me. It suddenly became difficult to draw in my breath.

Then, just as suddenly, its attention went to someone else and the heaviness of my soul went away. They selected three people who obediently and soundlessly accompanied them out the door; they not only knew there was no point in fighting, they were physically unable to do so due to some kind of control these alien beings hold over us while we are in their rooms. The door disappeared into the whiteness of the wall behind them. People sighed with relief and a few spoke quietly among themselves in various languages.

Something warm, wet, and slightly uncomfortable is in my nose. Wait … where am I? Why is everything now dark? What am I doing? A familiar feeling of panic begins to rise in my chest as my breathing intensifies. Something is not right. Then I hear something; it is the comforting sound of my husband lightly snoring, his breath gently rising and falling. Yes. I am home, I am in my own bed, I am safe. Thank God. Thank you, thank you, thank you, God. I gingerly touch my nose and something is wet and sticky. Another nosebleed. I slowly get out of bed, disoriented and dizzy, and go into the bathroom, shutting the door so the light won't disturb my husband. I switch on the glaringly bright light, revealing dark red blood smeared on the tip of my nose, with a trickle of fresh, brighter red running down to my chin, dripping onto my bare chest. Naked. Wait, where was I naked before? Wasn't I just somewhere else that was bright like this? A chill of fear washes over me. I hold a tissue to my nose and think of puppies. Flowers. Butterflies. Think of good things. Do not think of long slender silver tubes going up my nose. Think of happy things. Kittens. Bunnies. Do not think of shiny black eyes. Think of wildflowers in the spring.

*The air bristles and snaps with electricity, charged with an unseen presence. The distant hum of hundreds of bees drone in your ears, buzzing closer and closer until you are certain they must be flying directly into your brain. Your body becomes limp and heavy until even breathing is an effort. A singsong voice calls your name from far away in the distance, beyond the buzzing. It calls again, this time louder and more insistent. And again, now right next to your ear, slowly and deliberately, filled with purpose.*

*And that's how you know they are here. Fighting the utter terror rising in your throat, you open your eyes to see what you already know is there; an alien face so close to yours that it is almost touching your nose. Alien eyes staring into the depths of your being. —October 25, 2014*

\*\*\*

## Faces in the Night

Aliens are ... well ... *alien*. When you wake up in the middle of the night and a foreign face with huge shiny black eyes is staring directly into yours, the reptilian part of your brain reacts first and asks questions later. You try to yell and kick and scream and fight. Only you can't, because you have been paralyzed. You can move your eyes but you can't move your face away from this big ... this big ... BUG ... this big MONSTER. The gigantic bug eyes stare into your eyes, into your body, into your very soul, and they know your innermost self. This creature is doing some kind of mindreading trick and even though you

3

try your damnedest to close your eyes, to roll away, to kick, to punch, your body is heavy as lead and unresponsive to your commands. It is the most helpless and pathetic feeling I have ever experienced, and I have experienced it countless times in my life.

When something alien touches your life, touches your brain, you are never the same again. At a tender young age my reality was turned on its side and continued to teeter on the edge of a precipice, swaying between the sunshine of a normal life and the dark abyss of the terrifying unknown.

In the early 1990s I spent hours in the local library researching the paranormal, the occult, telepathy, alien abductions, dreams, basically whatever weirdness I could get my hands on. I didn't have access to the Internet at that time so the library was the place to go. I found a book called *Secret Life* by Dr. David Jacobs, which is a study of multiple alien abductions. It made me feel not so alone. In this excerpt from *Secret Life*,[1] Dr. Jacobs describes the staring procedure, which he calls the Mindscan:

## STARING PROCEDURES

Throughout the abduction, both as a way of communicating with the abductee and presumably, of examining and altering her mental and emotional state, the Beings stare deeply into the abductee's eyes. For instance, during the first moments of an abduction, often before the abductee has been transported to the UFO, an alien inexplicably stares deeply into an abductee's eyes. When the abductee is very excited or frightened during the abduction, an alien stares into her eyes, calming her. Staring can also alleviate an abductee's pain. However, the most profoundly affecting of the staring procedures is Mindscan.

---

## Mindscan

After the Small Beings complete the physical examination and implant the device, they stand back from the abductee. Then a Taller Being walks into the room. The Taller Being closely resembles the Small Being except that he is slightly taller, he might have subtly different facial features, he sometimes wears noticeable clothes, and he has an air of authority about him. He gives orders and the Small Beings obey. People often have strong and divided feelings about the Taller Being. Some hate him because he is clinical and brusque, and because he does "bad" things to them. Others feel he has more of a range of emotion and they can relate to him better than they can to the Small Beings. Abductees sometimes call him the doctor because of his demeanor and task. He is usually very businesslike, with a detached, matter-of-fact attitude …

At times the Taller Being will perform the physical exam himself, but Mindscan is the focus of his attention. Mindscan entails deep, penetrating staring into the abductee's eyes. Abductees commonly feel that data of some sort is being extracted from their minds. We do not know what the information is, how it is extracted, or what the Beings do with it. One abductee thinks that they transfer it to other beings' minds.

During Mindscan, the abductee lies on the table and the Taller Being stands next to her. He bends over and comes very close to the abductee, who may feel extremely frightened and threatened. He may even be close enough to touch foreheads with her … The Taller Being then gazes deeply into the abductee's eyes. His black eyes, which lack pupils, occupy a huge amount of space on his face. They are spellbinding, riveting. He locks eyes with the abductee. Even though she tries, she cannot close her eyes or take her eyes off his. Most abductees feel overwhelmed by the procedure.[1]

Dr. Jacobs concludes that the aliens are not pleasant or good beings and that they have malevolent intent and a negative influence on their contactees. This is where he and I diverge on our beliefs, but reading his book (several times) was extremely comforting to me, simply knowing I was not alone, though I strongly disagreed with his conclusions.

We are conditioned by Hollywood and other perpetrators of fear to cram what is "alien" into a very limited and narrow perspective. We are told what they should look like, what they should act like, where they probably come from. We are told that we should be very afraid of them and their motives. But what if I told you that is only one story, only one theory? What if I told you that reality, and at least one reality, *my* reality, is utterly different? What if I told you that their physics aren't the same as ours? Their fear is not the same as ours? Their thought processes are not the same as ours? They are here, in part, to try to comprehend the incomprehensible human being, much as we are trying to comprehend the incomprehensible alien.

They do not experience fear the way we do. It's why they don't understand why we freak out when they suddenly materialize in our (supposedly) warm safe bedrooms in the middle of the night, looking like giant bugs, paralyzing us and staring deeply into our eyes before zipping us through the wall. "Why is the human screaming? Why is the human desperately and ineffectively fighting this? We are simply studying the humans and will gladly impart technological and spiritual guidance and information, so why are they acting barbaric as we strip them of their clothing and insert our medical instruments into them?"

Their ignorance of our own experience is nearly as thorough as our ignorance of theirs. Though they are adept at communicating with us telepathically on a mental/intellectual/physical level, they simply cannot translate our raw emotions into anything they can recognize or understand. We are as perplexing and complicated to them as they are to us.

They had been working with me (and doubtless hundreds of other humans) on mutual trust and communication issues when I was at last allowed to become semiconscious on an exam table.

*Something happened that spooked me and I flailed my arms about wildly, smacking a small Grey in his torso and throwing him against the wall. He felt so frail and tiny, like a skinny squishy Pillsbury Dough Boy/Gumby. I hope I didn't hurt him. Crote* [an alien being I have come to know] *immediately placed his hand on my forehead and I blacked out, to awaken in my bed later. —August 19, 2002*

∗∗∗

I have interacted with aliens since I was a very young child, with my first memories being around age six. My mom said I had night terrors starting at age four. I may have been visited since I was born; I have witnessed human infants in the arms of otherworldly beings in my alien journeys. During the past forty-plus years of connecting, and I can only speak for myself here, we are beginning to understand each other. There are other contactees who have given up, who have asked the aliens to quit visiting them or prayed that they would stop, and they did. Some contactees have gone on heavy medications and/ or been locked away to make it stop. I pray that no one has committed suicide because of it, but I fear that some may well have because I can understand the sense of desperation that accompanies these experiences and the utter loneliness of not being able to tell even your spouse the absolute truth for fear that you are losing your mind and the fear of being put away in a mental institution, the fear of being ostracized from your loved ones.

But I know that aliens do abduct us. I have a decades-long history of it, and now is the time for me to come forward with what I know in the hopes of dispelling some of the fear, and moving the human race from its current situation rooted squarely in the grasp of fear into the everlasting arms of Love. Love is the natural state of the human being.

Love is the natural state of all life. Love is the motivation behind what the alien beings are doing to us, believe it or not. I will try to explain how I have come to this conclusion.

As an example of alien reality vs. our reality, I will describe their ships, or at least the ships I have been on that I can recall. We humans have decided that alien ships should be metallic and full of long metal hallways, barren of everything but instrument panels; just look at any sci-fi movie to see the similarities of their ships. However, no one told the aliens that's what ships should look like. They use lifeforms as part of their technology; they use plants as air generators and air purifiers; they use various beings with differing capabilities to perform tasks suited to their bodies and their abilities. Small crablike beings scuttle across floors, cleaning up spills and any debris left by the "dirty humans" as we are considered to be. Many humans will vomit with fear, or lose control of their bowels, and naturally we shed hair or drop articles of clothing or a toy or other thing we may be holding, and these crablike beings immediately creep in to soundlessly clean up. If nothing else, the aliens are extremely clean and sanitary.

The ships I've been aboard have no sharp pointed edges; everything is round, fluid, moving and changing like a living entity. The "walls" can be either solid, translucent, or completely clear depending on the requirements, and they can (and do) change instantly. Being aboard is disconcerting on many levels; it's like experiencing a continual carnival ride or bizarre nightmarish house of mirrors that you don't know is safe, you don't know when the ride will be over—if ever—and you can't quite get a grip on the dreamlike reality of it. Then there's that nagging sensation that you've been there before, the déjà vu of having done the same thing at other times with other people, and the sense of terror intensifies because that means it will probably continue to happen in the future.

I've been aboard ships that are similar to giant round aquariums, pulsating with life and light, filled with oxygen-producing seaweed. I floated around the different rooms in these ships, breathing the thick clear oxygen-rich fluid instead of air. Naturally the first few times they forced me to breathe in the thick watery atmosphere I completely panicked and feared for my life, but they would usually cause me to become unconscious and by the time I awoke, I was comfortably breathing in the oxygen-rich liquid. Once I wake up already aboard and already breathing the fluid, I am amazed at the ease with which I can float around in the buoyant atmosphere. The last visit I recall to one of these, I was not restrained on the ship and was given free rein to explore because, as our visits have continued, our relationship has evolved to the point where the aliens and I now trust each other, albeit guardedly. Inside this particular ship was a large storage place similar to an enormous warehouse, which glowed and pulsated with light and seemed to be filled with endless rows of clear vats filled with seaweed, swimming creatures, and giant pears in containers. Huge tubes connected to the ceiling acted as filtration systems for the vats. I wandered to the control room of this ship and floated, watching as we approached Earth. There were multiple aliens scurrying around, doing their jobs, and two who sat at the main control station in the center of the room. The entire front part of the ship was clear, and I was overwhelmed to watch the sky, the stars, the moon, and the utterly incredible beauty of the Earth as we silently approached. The control station was a pedestal-type table in the center of the room where two Grey aliens were seated. They communicated silently, nodding and occasionally gesturing to each other. Among the others in the control room were a small spidery being above the viewing window, controlling something with its multiple arms, another being or two on the ceiling doing something with their multitude of fingers. It seemed to be a crew of about eight beings in total, and there were several of us observing. I was the only human in that room at that time. I was completely enthralled with this experience and not at all frightened. This was about 2006 when my fears had at last begun to fade.

When they brought me home they landed this ship right in the middle of my living room. It was glowing amber, pulsating, as I stood next to it. Yes, it was an enormous ship while I was aboard, and, no, I didn't have a mansion that it landed in. Their physics are different from ours. They somehow made their ship about five feet tall and roundish, with a diameter of about five feet when they landed it in my living room. One moment I was floating inside the ship looking at my living room, breathing a heavy liquid oxygen, and the next I was standing outside of it, looking in, coughing out the clear liquid. I observed the ship from a disoriented state, an alien presence in my familiar living room. Different physics. Different realities. A Grey appeared next to me and, ignoring me, took a few moments to study my fifty-five-gallon aquarium. Next thing I knew, I was awakening in my own bed and it was morning.

\*\*\*

## Why Do They Come?

From what I've gleaned, aliens began studying us (humanity) in earnest after we dropped two atomic bombs on Japan in 1945. Up until that time we were an oddity, a curiosity, a rogue species perhaps, but benign and actually rather amusing. Suddenly we had become deadly not only to ourselves and the planet Earth, but to all surrounding realities and dimensions. We became children playing with matches and nukes. Things had become quite unstable and a call went out in the universe for assistance. Various species and communities got together to decide what to do. There were indeed those who felt the entire species, even the entire Earth, should be annihilated, as they believed that humans are not all that valuable in the grand scheme of things. But their voices were overruled in the interest of compassion and curiosity. How would things play out in the long run? Humans have amazing deep capabilities for intelligence, improvisation, and compassion, and incredible resilience in the face of danger. There are individuals throughout human history who have shown the way, been examples of compassion and love, but their teachings have been distorted and generally humans have continued on in their depravity and violence, sometimes even using those teachings to justify their terrorizing, murderous ways.

Aliens have always been in contact with individuals on the Earth, as long as humanity has existed. The aliens found it best to stay in the background, on the sidelines, else humans had a tendency to worship them as gods and they do not desire that. They kept one-on-one connections, and many chose to follow specific genetic lineages through the centuries, as time is not the same for them as it is for us. They can visit your great-great-grandfather and then come visit you in the same night. As far as I know I have not been on a ship together with one of my ancestors or descendants, though it's entirely possible that it has happened.

The aliens began early on, and continue to this day, to approach individual humans with knowledge, inspiration, and information. After 1945 they stepped up their interactions to help humanity swing the pendulum away from the tendencies of violence and selfishness and cruelty toward love, generosity, kindness, and compassion. Because we live in a free-will universe, it is entirely up to us as to what we do with the knowledge and information that is imparted to us. Since it took me personally nearly fifty years just to get past the fear of aliens, and now with the fear of going public I can guess that's one of the reasons why things are taking so long to change. And that's why I have been persuaded—um, forcefully urged—to write this book. I feel safe now lying in my bed and knowing that some nights they will come for me, for by now I am certain that they'll never hurt me; in fact, they have done some physical healing for me especially in regard to migraine headaches. They are now waking me up in the middle of the night with ideas as to what to write, how to present certain information, even names of publishers to submit to. I have a sense of urgency that this information needs to get out, and that humanity is at a crossroads: a *serious* crossroads that will affect humanity's future and the Earth's future. If even one person learns to accept the aliens without fear by reading this, then I've done what they are asking me to do, which is to teach others not to be afraid. Fear is our greatest enemy. Fear can cause someone to push the red button that sets off mutually assured nuclear destruction. Fear can bring down great nations. Fear can destroy men's souls. Fear is the opposite of love. Looking around today, *alien = fear* in most people's minds. I am here to tell you, that's Hollywood BS and not true, not in my experience. For me *aliens = friends. Aliens = love.* Yes, that's right. Love. Alien love, not human love, so it's a different experience altogether. They experience not only fear differently than we do; they also experience love differently than we do.

The aliens are here to gently guide us back toward love. Ironically, their very presence instills tremendous fear into us. It did for me for many years. The very thought of their existence gives most of us a chill down the spine. And yet they visit us. Millions of us. In their attempt to alleviate the fear, they replace actual memories of these visits with screen memories—you didn't see an alien with big eyes last night, you dreamed you saw an owl peering in your window. You weren't aboard a spaceship, you were riding in a glass elevator. You weren't on an exam table in a round white room with a doctor with huge black eyes, you were at a hospital in China. Do the aliens themselves implant these screen memories, or do our feeble human minds take something that is improbable, something bizarre, and attempt to make sense of it, to package the experience into something acceptable to our conscious mind? I do not know.

\*\*\*

After the Grand Meeting in our year 1945, many alien beings from various other planets volunteered to come and try to save the Earth, and save the humans from themselves. Most operate on the sidelines, staying secretive, and imparting their wisdom and knowledge either directly as they do to me, or indirectly, acting as guides, whispering information to scientists, researchers, doctors, environmentalists, politicians, and to regular everyday people to be inspired to take action to improve the world and to oppose negativity. A few brave souls volunteered to literally incarnate on the Earth, into a flesh-and-blood body, to work from within the system. Those who did had to agree to lose their memories of who they were and where they had come from so as not to interfere with humanity's free will. It was a difficult task, knowing they had an urgent mission but forgetting all about it upon birth. Some entities wished to keep their memories but incarnate on Earth as watchers. In order to do this, they had to incarnate into bodies that could not speak. Some of your nonverbal autistic children are such. Other aliens chose to be born into animal bodies, including domesticated cats and dogs. What better way to observe and infiltrate human lives than to live in the household, observing sexual habits, eating habits, toileting, communication? What better way to know the kindness of a human being if one is dependent on that human for food and care? Of course not all dogs and cats are actually alien beings incarnate, but a number of them are, and they are taking notes. We had a highly intelligent dog who would sit in a chair in the corner just like a person and calmly observe our family. My daughter used to say, "She's gathering data for the mothership."

The rest of us, who are just regular people but abductees, did agree to it on some level. I know many of you are screaming, "No way in hell did I agree to their probing and their terrifying abductions." It's hard to accept, I know, and if you insist that they stop, they will. But on some level, likely prior to being born, you did agree to it. This is a free-will universe, and they otherwise would not, could not, violate your free will.

They love us but they love the Earth more, and if we persist in destroying the Earth they will allow for a natural planetary cleansing to take place. They will absolutely not allow mutually assured destruction with nuclear weapons; they have already demonstrated that.2

\*\*\*

## Trust

There is a difference between the typical mishmash of everyday dreams that everyone has, where you are in school naked or running endlessly from a faceless monster, or flying above your house with the birds. They are vague, shadowy, and slip from waking consciousness soon after waking. These other "dreams," these alien experiences, are as real as the keyboard I now type on. They are every bit as real as my waking life; often filled with sounds, scents, and sights and colors that I have never experienced while awake. And they stay with me, especially if they contain some type of message that the aliens want me to remember. They will be recurrent, or they will simply intrude upon my waking mind with great vividness, forcing me to recall things I'd rather forget, especially the more unpleasant experiences. These "dreams" do not slip into the mists of wakefulness like true dreams do.

As a young child I desperately attempted to protect myself by having a nighttime ritual of surrounding myself with stuffed animals in my bed before I was tucked in. Surely the stuffed animals would protect me from the unspeakable horrors that lay in wait for me behind my closed eyelids. Dolls freaked me out—those unblinking eyes—but I loved all stuffed animals and definitely felt that they could protect me from the bug-eyed monsters. A big stuffed lion named Louie had to be next to my face. Maybe he could keep the staring eyes away from me. As I grew older I had live animals sleep with me but they never did protect me. I think they are "in on it" with the aliens (which is another big reason I believe the aliens mean no harm to us). As a young adult I realized it was hopeless when I saw my cat Sarah frequently accompanying me on my abductions, apparently willingly. She once jumped out of my arms, rubbed up against a Grey, and purred. I was devastated by the sense of betrayal I felt. But even my loyal dogs have accompanied me on these journeys.

I always knew these specific "dreams" were real, but my mother insisted on saying, "it's just a dream, dear" or "it's just your imagination," and then she would abruptly change the subject to homework or what's for dinner. It left me with an uncomfortable sense of desperately wanting to talk to someone who would really listen and not squirm uncomfortably or get a faraway look in their eyes. I needed to be validated; my experiences needed to be acknowledged. I needed to know that everything would be all right, but instead I got unspoken gestures and signs from the grownups in my life that everything was *not* all right. I learned at a tender age that trust is not so easy. How could

I trust Mommy to tell me the truth about something if she ignored the one subject that was most important to me? These experiences were terrifying me to my core, and her only response was a fake-sweet voice saying, "It's all just fine, dear, nothing but a bad dream." But I could see something troubling in her eyes, and my ability to trust anyone, especially loved ones, from a very young age was shattered. Because of this I have had difficulty with close relationships of all types, as there is the huge elephant in the room that only I know about, only I can see, and yet I cannot describe it or feel that I can tell anyone else it is there. This has affected all aspects of my life, most especially marriage. I was keeping a massively important aspect of my personal life secret from both of my husbands; yet I would angrily blow my top if they were less than honest with me about anything in their lives.

\*\*\*

## Exams

Ah, yes, the infamous examinations and anal probes. Most people, upon hearing "alien abduction," immediately think "anal probe." I can honestly tell you I have no recollection of ever having had one. No recollection, unfortunately, doesn't mean it never happened. But here's my theory: They do them on men only unless there is a specific medical reason to perform it on a woman. They apparently have an interest in harvesting our reproductive material, our eggs and sperm, and one way to harvest sperm from a man is by a procedure called prostate massage. The prostate is reached through the anus.

Here's an alternate theory about anal probes: When you take your dog or cat to the vet, what's one of the first things they do? They insert a small metal probe into the anus to get a stool specimen. By viewing the specimen under a microscope they can look for blood, parasites, and other abnormalities. The aliens are obviously interested in our environment and the toxins we are pumping into it. They may well be checking stool for evidence of toxicity. In fact, the whole abduction experience could be likened to what our scientists do with wild animals: Sedate the beast and take it from its native habitat, do a full medical evaluation including weight, measurements, blood samples, stool sample, and other relevant studies, then tag it for further follow-up and release it back into the wild while it is still partially or fully asleep. These are dangerous wild animals that would harm or kill our scientists if they did not sedate them. What's the difference between that and what the aliens do to us? They probably even tag us so they can follow us as we move to new locations—which abductees do more often than the average person, perhaps in a subconscious attempt to get away from the aliens. This theory came to me one night:

*Heard the familiar buzzing in my ear again, this time the left. I know that it's a tracking device. And why not? For decades now we have trapped animals—everything from sea turtles to salmon, polar bears to alligators—drugged them, measured, weighed, examined, taken blood samples and stool samples, checked the sex and sometimes even relocated them after fitting them with tracking devices before releasing them. Once in a while a specimen is kept for a zoo or to reproduce in a controlled environment—or, if considered a threat, even killed.*

*Why wouldn't those who visit us, whether from another planet, or from inside Earth, or from our future or from another dimension—do the very same thing to us? Why not? —August 24, 2005*

In that vein of thought, many have accused aliens of the cattle mutilations done around the country, with the belief that they are checking our cattle for environmental toxins or some other type of study. I do not believe the aliens are responsible for cattle mutilations. They live in peace and harmony, with respect for all living creatures including plants and animals. Sure they scare the hell out of us, but not intentionally, and they are actively learning how *not* to scare us. Killing cattle would not make sense to them. They have the means to do any necessary studies on the animal while it is alive. I've witnessed many cats and dogs accompanying their owners on ships and in exam rooms; it seems that our dogs and cats fully accept the aliens. I've also seen alien pets. The aliens love and respect life and would not do anything that horrific to a gentle, peaceful, vegetarian cow. Our government and corporations, however, are not always so ethical.

By the end of 2005 I had made my peace with the fact that I am indeed visited by alien lifeforms and that they will not hurt or kill me. They've had plenty of opportunities in the past decades to have done so. Not only have they not hurt me, but they have provided healing of mind and body for me on many occasions. By 2005 they had learned to give me advance notice when a visit was coming, so I wouldn't be caught off guard and scream horrifically. They would forewarn me with a buzzing in my ear as I prepared for bed, or sometimes a voice telling me, "we are coming." Sometimes I could sense their presence as early as dinnertime, and waited for the announcement. It didn't always come, but when it did they were true to their word and came for me. I worked hard at accepting that this was my fate and that I had a great deal to learn from them. They, in turn, were learning from me, such as how not to frighten the humans!

*Was awakened by a "rod" descending from above my head— silver, about 1 inch diameter, hollow, coming 3 feet down to my forehead from the ceiling* [as I lay on my back in my bed]. *I did not scream, was fascinated. Sensed presences around. Not hostile.* [I then went on to describe the instrument as hollow and black inside, the part approaching me cut on the diagonal and aiming for my third eye. I described the instrument as shiny, yet tarnished, old-looking.] *Went back to sleep. Awoke with HORRIBLE headache unlike others (not migraine, not sinus, not sick, not toxic) going from top of spine, spreading through head on both sides, culminating in forehead. Feels like brain won't fit in skull. Enormous pressure.*
*—December 11, 2005*

It is not usual for me to awaken in bad pain after an alien visit, but it does sometimes happen. I accept that for some reason this is necessary. They do not intentionally inflict pain, but in the case above they were opening my third eye and I had some resistance—there were things I literally didn't want to "see"—so it was my own resistance that caused the intensity of pain.

> 12/11/05
>
> Was awakened by a "rod" descending from above my head - silver, about 1" diameter, hollow, coming 3 feet down to my forehead from the ceiling.
>
> silver → descending movement
> shiny yet → em. 3 ft.
> tarnished, old → black inside - (hollow?)
> looking → cut on diagonal
>
> apt 3 ft
> me in bed
> aiming for my 3rd eye
>
> I did not scream, was fascinated. Sensed presences around. Not hostile.
>
> Went back to sleep. As I awoke with HORRIBLE headache unlike others (not migraine, not sinus, not sick, not toxic) going from top of spine, spreading thru head, both sides, culminating in forehead. Feels like brain won't fit in skull. Enormous pressure.

I had a cystoscopy—a procedure where the doctor inserts an instrument into the bladder to look around and see what the problem is—around 1990. Due to insurance reasons he had to do the procedure in his office without anesthesia (which I will never submit to again, that hurt unbelievably!). He told me I did not appear to have any infection but did have severe scarring in my urethra, the tube that leads from the bladder to outside the body. I told him that when I was six years old I had another cystoscopy in which the doctors told my mother they had to "stretch my bladder" because it was very tiny. He shook his head, saying this was more severe scarring than what would be present from a surgery done twenty-some years ago. I then told him I had suffered from multiple repeat bladder infections throughout my life. Again he seemed confused and said no, infections would not have left this type of surgical scarring. It was incidents like this, for which neither the doctor nor I had an explanation, that were slowly causing me to accept that the things going on in my dreams were, in fact, real.

Probably one of the most awful aspects to abduction is the realization that it occurs in family lineages, so it is likely occurring to my child as well. When my daughter was five years old there were several suspect occasions with respect to her nightclothes. Once I tucked her into bed wearing her pajamas, yet she awoke the next morning with the pajamas inside out. Another time she went to bed dressed, but awoke

18

naked with the pajamas very neatly folded at the foot of her bed. The most disturbing time was when she awoke wearing a nightgown *that wasn't hers*. I had never seen it before, and she had gone to sleep in PJs, not a nightgown. There were no strangers or guests in our home, and her bedroom was right next to mine. If there is anything more horrifying than having them come for me, doing examinations on me, it's knowing they have come for my baby.

\*\*\*

## Screen Memories

Our frail human brains can only handle so much extreme input before they have some kind of breakdown. We know this. The aliens know this. As such, we are given "screen memories" to mask the actual incidents that happen to us. Whether screen memories are given to us by the aliens to help us forget what we have experienced and therefore keep them incognito, or whether our own minds make up strange dreamlike events in a wild attempt to make sense of that which is nonsensical, I do not know.

Common screen memories for aliens with big eyes include seeing or dreaming of owls, deer, or people with large sunglasses. Screen memories for being on a ship can be round rooms, movie theaters, unusual cars, submarines, classrooms. Screen memories for the physical exams can involve unusual hospitals, "Asian" doctors (short with large dark eyes), schoolroom volunteers for anatomy class, even autopsy dreams. Here's an example of a screen memory dream that includes seeing a possible sexual encounter with other abductees:

*I was in China, and someone next to me (in some kind of a rickshaw?) took me to look in the front of a store where someone was talking about prostitution. I went inside and was surrounded by short Asian people. There was a window where a prostitute was sitting. A Chinese man put down $30 in American money and went up the steps to see her. She very roughly threw him down and got on top of him. He* was very muscular and had long hair in a braid down his back. The prostitute said, "I will take two hours with him," when the next man tried to give her money. We all watched through the window as she had sex with him. She turned her back, and her skin was pale, purplish, and she had spots on her butt cheeks.

A man wearing coveralls and carrying a clipboard asked me if my daughter had had her baby yet. Then we all went out front and the guy with the coveralls was looking up at the sky. I saw a UFO that looked like a satellite that he was watching. It came down and landed on the grass by a pool. When the man touched it, it looked like a drum set with keyboards. He touched it very carefully, especially the Congo drums. A piece of the top broke off and I could see that it was made of a type of Styrofoam so that it could float. Then we had to rush away and I was mad at my husband that he wouldn't go with me. I escaped with others in a small car.

--- Woke up with very stiff neck and marks like :// on the inside of my left ankle, very sore. I had awakened at 3 a.m. with a voice telling me "something is very wrong," with great concern. I got up to check the house, feeling very uneasy. The dogs were asleep but the cat was watching me. My head had stabbing pains. I went back to sleep with an ice pack on my head and had the above dream. —August 5, 1999

The above dream was a premonition dream in two ways. First, my daughter had a baby in 2009, but back in 1999 she was single and very much planned on staying that way and never having children. Second, my husband and I divorced in 2005 and in the dream *"I was mad at my husband that he wouldn't go with me."*

\*\*\*

Had incredible excruciating headache again yesterday—fourth day in a row and each exponentially worse—last night I was watching TV in the living room. At 9:58 when the show was over I went and got an ice pack from the freezer, grabbed my pillow and headed for bed. As

*I walked through the dining room—BAM I had a gap in awareness!! I was in an unfamiliar, dark place. Very dark. There were slight ribbons of bright light vertically. I screamed instinctively.*

*Then I heard my husband's voice. "Lie down." He sounded very close.*

*"But ..." I gasped. "I don't know where I am!!"*

*"You're in our bedroom," bless his patient heart.*

*I still didn't feel like I was in our bedroom. I focused on the shafts of vertical light, two of them, and they slowly rotated around until they were horizontal and I could recognize that they were beams from the streetlight shining underneath the bedroom drapes. It was as though I had been floating in midair, sideways, causing the vertical lightstrips to look horizontal. Yet I didn't have the feeling of movement, only the sensation that the light itself was moving. I tentatively reached out my hands in the dark and took baby steps until I felt the firm corner of our dresser, and then reality slammed into place like a door locking and I knew exactly where I was. What's odd is that the ice pack I had just taken from the freezer was now warm. And instead of 10 pm, the bedroom clock read 10:23. Where had I been for those 20-some minutes while my ice pack thawed out?*

*I went on to dream about being in a weird room with others in which we were being examined, checked for heart rate, thoughts, etc.*
*—August 17, 2001*

\*\*\*

## The Lens of Fear

We have been taught to view the world through the eyes of fear. Nightly news swirls with tension over wars, viruses, terrorists, political wrongdoing ... be afraid, be very afraid. Be afraid of strangers, be afraid of people of another race, people from a different country, wild animals. My five-year-old grandson wanted to watch a video about dinosaurs so we searched YouTube but all we could find were gruesome, neck-biting, bloody, fight-to-the-death dinosaur scenes, even coming from the Discovery Channel! There were no videos of vegetarian brachiosaurs grazing the primitive grasslands, living in peaceful herds. I suppose that would be considered boring.

I am guilty of seeing through the eyes of fear as well. Walking my dog at dusk I see a hooded teenager coming toward me on a skateboard. Instinctively I rein in the dog and step off the sidewalk onto the grass, only to see the young man stop, pick up his skateboard, and carry it under his arm as he passes me, nodding and smiling as he quietly says, "excuse me," before stepping back on the board after he passes me. I had fallen back on traditional stereotypes and did not look at this youth through the eyes of love. If a dog runs toward you, off leash, what is your first reaction? That it wants to attack you or play with you? If you are alone on a dark street and a dark-skinned man approaches, do you grab onto your purse? True, dogs sometimes do attack and people do sometimes get robbed; but the majority of people are good and want to be good. Most dogs want to chase and play. The world, the universe, is a good and loving and safe place. If someone is going to harm me, my worrying about it all day isn't going to change their behavior. We attract what we fear so if we believe the world is a terrifying, out-of-control chaotic dangerous place, then we will attract confirmation of that in our world. Our ears will prick up when such confirmation is overheard, perhaps ignoring the previous news story about the Good Samaritan who raised thousands of dollars to help a family whose house had caught fire, and instead only hearing the story about school violence.

We have been force-fed fear of the world for as long as we can remember. As a kid I sat raptly watching the Mutual of Omaha Wild Kingdom specials each week, in which animals fought and stalked and tore each other to pieces. "This is what nature does," they were telling us subconsciously. "Be afraid of nature. Be afraid of the animals. Don't go out in the jungle alone; hell, don't ever go to the jungle at all! And don't go anywhere alone!" Then it became known via a Canadian

Broadcasting Corporation show, *The Fifth Estate,* in an episode titled "Cruel Camera," that many of the gut-wrenching scenes of animal cruelty and nature's cruelty were actually falsely set up for the sake of the camera.3 We now know, thanks to YouTube, that many animal species interact just beautifully, as in the cases of a mother cat nursing an orphaned bunny, a chimpanzee playing with a puppy, a hippo and a tortoise, Koko the gorilla tickling Robin Williams, or any number of unique interspecies bondings. There are also scenes of gazelles grazing peacefully near lion prides, safe in the knowledge that the lions are not hungry at present. Unlike humans, they do not kill for sport or pride or trophies; they only kill for food and do not kill when not hungry. The perception of nature as terrifying is slowly but thankfully evolving.

\*\*\*

# Chapter 2

## Dreams

*I refuse to dream about that. That is the domain of my subconscious, and there is one thing to do and that is to seal off the evil monster-ridden haunts of my mind and dream about goodness. Dream about love. Dream about sunshine. Dream about flying, free to experience the joy that is unlimited in the surreal reality. There is only one thing to do and that is kill the monsters and the darkness and dream about laughter and brightness. —June 1986*

I have been plagued by "bad dreams" all my life. My earliest memory, at age six, was of being sound asleep, warm and cozy in my safe bed, when I felt someone staring at me. I opened my eyes and there was a face, a large nonhuman face, so close to mine that my nose was nearly touching it. But it didn't have a nose with which to touch mine. It only had enormous black eyes, shiny bug-like eyes that locked with my eyes and refused to let go. Those eyes were staring past my eyes, into my head, into my brain, into my very being. Those eyes held my physical body in paralysis while they read all my hopes, my fears, my deepest secrets. And when they finally released the paralysis my mind was stripped of its humanity and all that was left to do was scream. There were no words left; the eyes had taken them away. Just scream like a wild terrified animal; scream until I somehow regained my conscious awareness of who I am, what I am, where I am.

You know when you feel something on your arm, glance down, and see a big hairy spider crawling on you? You yell and fling your arm wildly before your brain engages the thought to take a more rational approach. It's like that when you wake up to a seven-foot-tall praying mantis leaning over you. You scream bloody murder. It's instinct; it's the reptilian part of your brain kicking in and you can't do anything but scream.

I remember as a teenager running, breathlessly screaming down the hallway toward my parents' bedroom with something grabbing and snapping at my heels; a monstrous presence breathing down the back of my neck, heart pounding as if it would burst. It was sheer terror. My mother would allow me to fall asleep on the floor next to her bed, but my dad was angry and I remember him yelling that "something is very wrong with a sixteen-year-old girl who still has to sleep with her parents." My mom, though problematic in other areas of my life, staunchly defended me here; she was so compassionate about my experiences it caused me to wonder if she had experienced them herself. "It's just a dream, dear," she'd say soothingly as she stroked my forehead. "None of it is real." But I knew about regular dreams; they are nonsensical, flimsy, scattered images of the mind; normal everyday dreams of showing up for school naked or falling off a cliff or flying high over a city. Even as a young child I knew the difference between reality and fantasy or dreams, and these were no dreams. These experiences, these alien visitations, these quote-unquote dreams, are vivid and realistic and most are etched into my brain as unforgettable, unlike everyday dreams, which fade away in the morning light. I've seen colors that are not seen here on Earth. I've heard music and other sounds that I've never heard while awake. All my senses are vividly engaged during these experiences, including touch and taste and smell. The memories of these times are as vivid as the real-life memories of the day I had my baby, or my first day of school, or the day I got married; especially the ones "they" want me to remember.

In my family this was considered to be a shameful secret so it was never discussed. Not among ourselves and certainly not with a doctor or neighbor or friend. It was a dirty little secret; something was wrong with Donna, and we mustn't let anyone else know, which of course only added to my burden. I was terrified not only of the monsters, but terrified also when invited to sleepovers that it would happen then. My first husband yelled at me to stop and told me I needed to see a psychiatrist. My poor daughter learned at an early age that if she came into Mommy's room, Mommy might start screaming and flailing about. I don't know what the child felt alone in her room, listening to Mommy's screams. I ask her now that she's an adult and she claims to have little memory of it; yet when her two-year-old recently awoke from a sound sleep screaming, unable to be consoled, my daughter immediately called me to ask about night terrors and if they are hereditary (yes, they are), and I knew she was very concerned. My second husband was wonderful—for the first few years. He would rub my back, sit and hug me as I trembled, speak in calm low tones to me, let me nestle against his powerful chest until I stopped crying and shaking and got back to sleep. But after about seven years he started losing patience—really can anyone blame him? He started saying, "Shut up already!" or "Good God, you're going to give me a heart attack, screaming like that in the middle of the night." Sometimes I don't recall the experience unless my screams are piercing enough to wake me from the deep trance I seem to be in. He would tell me in the morning, "You did it again last night," and I thought he was teasing me. Then he'd say, for example, "You were in the closet screaming, yelling that we have to pack and leave. You were throwing your shoes at me." Now I really didn't believe him. He beckoned for me to come to his side of the bed—where my mismatched shoes littered the floor and edge of the bed.

To this day as I write these experiences and in my dream journal I still call them "dreams," but I put that in quotes as a way to distinguish the difference between these experiences and actual dreams. What else do I call them? I don't like the word "abduction," as it is representative of violence and a violation of free will. Others call them "experiences" or "visits" or "contacts," but those doesn't really seem to fit either. So for lack of a better word I continue to use "dreams." I seem to lack the vocabulary to describe this alternate reality, the absolutely bizarre world in which six-inch-tall fairies and seven-foot-tall insects interact with one another and with me; they silently observe me or grab me out of my comfortable warm bed in the middle of the night to do unspeakable experiments on me, or teach me to fly a spaceship, or take me to other worlds where I have other families who are surprised and thrilled to see me.

Sometimes the "dreams" remain in silent submission in my subconscious mind until something happens to unlock the memory, some kind of trigger; for example, swimming pool lights. I was six years old when my parents decided I needed to learn how to swim. They took me to a large, Olympic-sized community pool, to a class with other kids my age. The pool terrified me. Not the actual pool, not the water, not the fear of drowning, but the lights in the pool. Lights underwater. They triggered memories in me, terrible awful memories. I went to the first two lessons, but when it came time for me to put my face underwater and open my eyes and look at those lights, I absolutely refused. I screamed like my arm was being cut off. I cried and hollered and yelled until my mother finally relented and took me home, embarrassed. She couldn't understand what I was so afraid of—all the other kids were doing it. The water was warm. The teacher was nice. What was my problem? I couldn't tell her how the pool terrified me, spooked me, scared me to a depth my six-year-old self could neither identify nor verbalize. I couldn't explain to her how it triggered powerful repressed memories of being forced underwater in a similar-looking pool, being forced to breathe in the sticky liquid, the terror as it went up my nose and down my throat and into my lungs while the whole time a big underwater light was watching me, testing me, taunting me. That pool, that other "dream" pool, was about three times the size of the community pool. It was black. The liquid was clear but the bottom and sides were black, making the clear thick liquid appear black so that all that showed was the lights. Rows of big round glowing lights under the black water.

I wasn't alone at the black pool; there were many kids of different ages standing around the sides and edges of the pool. One at a time we were forced to jump in. Some swam to the other side while others, myself included, had to go down. Down, down. Something on top of my head forced me down until I couldn't hold my breath anymore, and in blind panic I opened my eyes to see the light, the giant round light, as I gasped in the liquid and realized I was still awake, still aware, still conscious. Breathing in the fluid. Staring at the light.

When I was allowed out of the pool I had to cough and spit and sputter until all the fluid was out of my lungs. No one was there to calm me down or console me. I was a little child and I was terrified; I had just technically drowned. And they just stared at me and used their lights to watch me.

After I got used to breathing in the liquid, I was able to stand poolside and jump in voluntarily. Well, that is if you could call it volunteering; I knew if I didn't do it I would be forced, so I did it myself. I can still recall the inside shaking shivering feeling of horror as I stood at the edge of the black water with the shiny round lights and realized it was a shape down there, it was a round thing with lights, like maybe a fat submarine. Or a black airplane with no wings. And I had to jump in, breathe in the sticky liquid, and go down to look at the lights on the thing. It was some kind of a test. They were testing me, and I wanted to do well for them. I wanted to please them, I wanted them to like me. And so I bit down on my fear and jumped into the black pool with the round bright lights. But Mom and Dad could not make me jump into the pretty blue community pool; I knew they would not force my head underwater until I couldn't breathe. To this day I am fine swimming underwater in the ocean with the possibility of sharks; I am fine swimming in fresh Florida springs with the possibility of alligators; but swimming underwater near a swimming pool light will still cause a weakness in my belly and a shakiness in my soul.

\*\*\*

## Disasters and Destruction

One of the reasons most people fear alien contact is the visions of earthly destruction and disaster that they bring. The aliens use huge movie-type screens, far more realistic than the best IMAX theater, to show horrific scenes of nuclear wars, simultaneous volcano eruptions, massive tsunamis, off-the-scale earthquakes, and just about any and every other kind of disaster one can imagine. Why would they do this if they are benevolent?

I very clearly recall standing in the control room of a ship, hovering out past our moon. I was shown massive simultaneous explosions over our planet's surface. I screamed and cried in terror and begged the aliens to help, but they were cold and unyielding. At the time I thought it was really happening right then. Over the years I've been shown hundred-foot-high tidal waves washing over the beach in Santa Barbara; volcanoes destroying large cities; the Pacific Ocean circling the Los Angeles basin, swirling away people, property, and buildings. The intensity of the feeling of utter desolation I experienced with the thought of losing my planet, or huge portions of it, are something I will always carry with me.

For those who remember, there was quite a bit of hype and fear surrounding the dawning of the year 2000 (Y2K). Computers all over the world were supposed to crash, leaving electric systems, gas pumps, banks, and other systems all over the world rendered useless. The launch codes for the entire world's nuclear arsenal could potentially go off, destroying the planet. Regardless of what happened, life would never be the same, we were all certain of that. I spent that New Year's Eve with my husband, my daughter and her boyfriend, and good friends, having drinks and trying not to think of the devastation about to descend upon the world—if there still was to be a world. In the end, of course, not a thing happened.

The dreams leading up to this much-prophesied event were no less frightening. Whether the aliens were feeding into my fear, or feeding my fear, I am uncertain. I know they were still at the point where they were experimenting with the human emotions of fear and terror, and what better time than now, when the whole world was on edge about the impending millennium? Here's an example of one of my dreams of that era, which seemed to center mostly on nuclear devastation:

*I had to go prepare for the end of the world. My husband was not coming with me. I had just given birth to twins but had to leave the babies.*

*I was in the desert and at first there were hardly any people; then later there were a lot. I tried to join up with another couple but they went on without me. I was trying to find a safe place to nestle in the rocks.*

*Then a bunch of people were at a beach, watching for a space shuttle/fireworks show. There were lots of people. I tried to get comfortable on the sand. Some people crowded around me and a guy sat behind me so I could lean on his knees. It felt wrong to be that close to someone who wasn't my husband. My belongings got buried under the sand and I was upset, but a girl said, "Why bother?" because I knew we were all going to die anyway.*

*Then the show started. It was a gigantic space shuttle and it turned so we could see inside. There were robotic people doing stuff and everyone watching was amazed. I was sickened that all that money had been spent on the space shuttle and the space program, when people were going to die.*

*I woke up so sad and depressed, and worried that it meant my husband was going to leave me. I've been teary eyed all day. —* December 22, 1999

My husband had had an affair earlier that year with a much younger woman and had gotten her pregnant, and she had the baby a few days before this dream so it's possible the sorrow, fear, and tears are representative of my sorry state of mind in those days. However, I bring it to this book because of the space shuttle, which obviously was a screen memory for a different kind of space vehicle, driven by robotic entities. We were also waiting for this particular space shuttle to do a special kind of fireworks show, whatever that might indicate. I mention my husband's part in this because the aliens do play on emotions from our daily lives in order to study us—I was going through a horrifically emotional period so they were adding dreams to emphasize those emotions of loss, fear, babies, and concern for the future. I do not believe they are intentionally cruel. They do not fully understand human emotions; this is what they are trying to learn. Instead, they are researching us and our emotional reactions both in reality and in the dream state. They are simply doing their jobs, which is to ascertain what human emotions are about, and they are clearly confused by our depth and breadth of emotions.

I believe the extreme depths of destruction they show us are to purposely scare us into action to save our Earth. They love the Earth and care about its well-being. They do not understand how humans can live on such a beautiful planet and treat it so horrifically. They have shown me that Earth is a living entity with emotions of its own, albeit different from ours, but that the destruction we do to the Earth affects all of the lifeforms on her, including ourselves. We cannot continue to foul our own nest and expect no repercussions. I know that as a direct result of alien interactions I have become an avid environmentalist and animal activist. After watching your planet being destroyed in front of your eyes, you look upon it quite differently when you awaken the next morning to find that Earth is still here and you have the potential to make a difference.

\*\*\*

As I finally came to terms with the fact that these experiences were real, I began getting recurrent messages that it was up to me to help begin spreading the word that the aliens are here to help us help ourselves, and that others can learn to see them and trust them as well.

*I was standing outside in a field on a hill, and heard 3 or 4 large old planes coming, the kind with props so they were loud, slow, rumbling. They got my attention so I looked up to see them coming over the horizon, closely followed by dozens? or hundreds? of bright green UFOs; round with yellow etched markings or lights on the undersides. I was awed, not scared. Then a voice in my head—a commanding voice—said,* **We need you. You are one of our Ambassadors. You must tell people not to be afraid. Now is your time to step up. You have been called.** *—December 29, 2009*

*I got into an Army Jeep and headed north up the coast; it was an area like Cedar Key [Florida] or Panama City on the Gulf Coast where I saw a UFO on the beach. I pulled over and ran toward it. It was nearby, about two feet in diameter, humming, rimmed with red lights. I was so excited. Then dozens more (or hundreds) came in from the Gulf to greet me.*

*I heard shots and looked up to see military men shooting at them, angry and fearful. Their bullets bounced off but I felt like I needed to teach them and yelled at them to stop. Most did.*

*Then two kids joined me plus two other kids, including a boy in diapers and an older girl. I was frantic that they'd get shot. My sister joined me too. I tried desperately explaining to the military men to not be afraid. Then one of the UFOs "beamed" me inside where I'd be safe. Even though they're small, our physics don't apply to them so it was large inside. I think my sister and the kids were also brought in, but I was awakened then. —December 5, 2009*

I find it interesting that I chose to say "awakened" rather than woke up. By 2009 I was fully cognizant of the aliens and their visits and I was not afraid. I was living in California by 2009 but still dreaming of being in Florida. Our time and space and physics do not apply to them, as they have told me numerous times. It was toward the end of the first decade of the new millennium that I started receiving messages that I needed to tell the military that the UFOs were the good guys, and not to shoot, even though their weapons were useless against them anyway. It seemed more important that I reach individual soldiers so that they would not be afraid. I was speaking to individuals when I was brought aboard during this dream. That, combined with frequent messages that I am meant to be some kind of ambassador, made me realize that I was eventually going to have to speak out about these experiences. The thought of that scared me more than the aliens did.

I now accept my fate and understand that the "monsters" and their big black eyes do not mean me any harm. Honestly if they were going to kill me or harm me in any way, they have had decades in which to do so. On the contrary, they have come to my aid at night after surgery, or during migraine headache attacks, and they have alleviated some of my pain. They do not understand pain the way humans do; they do not understand fear the way humans do; they do not understand time the way humans do. They have put in a great deal of effort to learn about us and why we are the way we are. They still don't understand us very well, but they are earnest in attempting to learn; just as I don't understand them very well but am equally intent on learning about them. After all they are alien. They're not like us. There is so much to learn.

*We are here with you now. Do not fret the small trivial unimportant matters. It is with a great sincerity that we are amongst you.* —*August 26, 1996*

*A holy woman from India was bedside with a small child. She was explaining to me and others that the child had a brain tumor, but that sometimes tumors are deliberate implants that need to fully expand and integrate into the body before they work right.*

*Some were listening to her; others (my sister, my mom) either weren't paying attention or didn't understand.*

*I know she was speaking indirectly to me because of the tumors I've had removed, particularly the skull tumor; and now there is one deep in my hip that would be nearly impossible to remove and that will be hopefully less painful for me, so that I will allow it to remain and to fulfill its destiny within me.*

*I did not understand its purpose (or else I can't remember) but she did explain it carefully to me.* —*August 6, 2001*

I've had many tumors removed in my lifetime, most notably in 1997 a large skull tumor on my right temporal area that had to be removed and replaced with a plate made of bone cement (methyl methacrylate), attached with small plates and eight titanium screws. It was benign and there was no explanation for where it came from; I had not had an injury there. It just started growing when I was in my early twenties, and by the time I was thirty-nine years old it was very large and painful. I was terrified to have my head cut open but had no choice at that time as it was impinging on one of the nerves connected to my right ear and I would soon lose all hearing in that ear if it was allowed to keep growing. Also the migraine headaches associated with the tumor were really severe and increasing in number and strength. Unfortunately, the surgery made the headaches worse instead of better and changed my life for the worse as it resulted in left arm weakness and memory glitches and constant pain.

Ironically I had my ovaries and tubes removed in October 2001, only two months after the above "dream." The surgery was scheduled right away after my pelvic ultrasound, on the possibility that it was ovarian cancer, so I believe that at the time of this "dream" I was unaware of the multiple cysts and tumors on my ovaries and tubes. Just prior to this "dream" I had been diagnosed with a bone tumor inside my upper femur and that was what the dream was referring to. This particular tumor was never subjected to surgery and I have not had x-rays done of that area since, so I am guessing it was able to fulfill its destiny within

me as the holy woman described, and I have not developed any more tumors since that time. This dream offers a new way of looking at benign tumors.

*∗∗∗*

*Suddenly I was sitting next to a pilot in a weird helicopter in that it was round and hummed instead of having rotors, and I didn't need to be strapped in. I sat to the right of the pilot and asked her how she could see and not bump into things, because there was no windshield; instead there was a curved control panel. It was a beige/tan color with colored hieroglyphs on it. There was a very small viewing window just in front of her. She said, "I can't," and then the whole front panel became see-through and I could see trees rushing past and houses and power lines, and I saw that we were going very low, only a few feet off the ground. We seemed to be going several hundred miles per hour, zipping past things. Just as I wondered how we weren't hitting things, we bumped something.*

*Then a noise brought me to consciousness and I said something in my sleep. My husband said, "I hear it too." Was it a UFO? I know I was flying! —undated, but sometime between October 2000 and February 2005 when I lived in a particular house.*

I recall being frightened when the windshield went clear, as we were so low to the ground and flying through a densely populated area. Somehow it was made clear to me that we passed *through* solid objects due to the speed at which we were moving. It was only when I allowed my fear of hitting things to come to the forefront that we actually did hit something, and that resulted in me being unceremoniously dropped off at my bed, hearing the humming sound fading away into the night. But my husband heard it too!

*∗∗∗*

35

## Up Your Nose with a Rubber Hose

There have been countless dreams and experiences in which the aliens inserted a tube or instrument up one or both of my nostrils. Sometimes the instrument is clear, like aquarium tubing; other times it is a shiny silver rod. I had multiple other experiences of things being put up my nose, and when it involves their shiny silver instruments I nearly always wake up with a nosebleed. There have been instances where I've been held standing in some kind of boots that prohibit me from being able to step away or move, and then the clear tubes are inserted and I am forced to breathe in a type of salty water. This is terrifying and suffocating. I can feel the cool salty water going up my nose, down into the back of my throat, and burning slightly as it seeps into my lungs. I cannot scream. I cannot run. My arms are frozen to my sides. My head is held in place by large invisible hands or clasps or some type of fixation device so that it is immobile. And the watery substance is pumped slowly up my nose, down my throat, into my lungs. I keep breathing, gasping and panicking, but breathing, until I eventually realize that this is some kind of breathable fluid and is not hurting me. After the first few times this happened I knew intellectually that I would survive this but that doesn't stop the instinctual fear of drowning from kicking in, doesn't stop that blind panic from infusing every cell of my being.

At last I was taken to a place where I needed to undergo the fluid breathing, and I then understood that the previous times had been a preparation for visiting this particular place. I stepped out of their ship and was in a pink place. The sky was pink, the ground was dark pink. The air had a pink tint. The clouds were pink-peach. I was led to a white castle-type structure and shown stairs that went downward. A clear water-like substance, but slightly thicker than water, filled the room below. I slowly stepped down, and by the third step I was ankle-deep in this fluid. I was fearful to go any deeper, but the aliens who accompanied me went ahead of me, dunking themselves in the "water," showing me it was not to be feared. They sent me mental images of the times I had breathed in such "water" and been just fine. This was the place they were preparing me to see. So I took another step, and another, until I was chest-deep. They were not pushing or pulling me, and I knew this had to be a free-will choice on my part. I was free to leave. But I looked around the large open room under the water and it was full of people, human people and alien people all interacting in a party-type environment. I could hear a muffled type of music, unlike any music here on Earth. They were also eating some unusual looking foods. The room was filled with large white floor-to-ceiling pillars, around which the people gathered. The music seemed to be coming from the pillars. At the other end of the room was an arched doorway through which people came and went. I felt drawn to that doorway, so against my body's screaming desire to run away, I took another step down. The water level was up to my chin and I had to hold my head upward a little to keep it from going into my mouth. My accompanying alien friends were very excited; I could sense it. This was something of a test for me as well as for them. I slowly lowered my head and allowed some of the liquid to seep into my mouth. It had no taste or smell, was clear, and seemed to be the same temperature as my body; in other words, as comfortable as it could be to have to willingly allow into my lungs. I drank some in and then in a leap of faith, like a small child into a pool, I swam forward and allowed it to go up my nose as I deeply inhaled. There was no pain, there was no fear, but exhilaration! This is what they wanted me to do but they had not expected me to embrace it, and I realized I caught them off guard as I swam through the room, taking everything in. This is how they seem to swim through our atmosphere with their finned feet. They did not expect me to be so brave. I believe this was a turning point in our relationship, and I gained a sense of admiration and respect from them, whereas in the past I had sensed disdain from them.

I do wish I had written this experience down but it was so real, so wild, I just knew I would never forget it. It happened while I was living at the home I was in from October 2000 until February 2005, so it was sometime during that time frame. That is also the period in which we established a relationship of mutual trust rather than that of fearful victim and terrifying abductors. It was the beginning of a true friendship.

Around 1996 I had a vivid dream in which I was aboard a ship with my entire extended family. We were each having clear plastic tubes put into one nostril and most of us were fighting it and being held down. Finally, Crote came over and took me to a window, in which I could see the Earth below. We were quite a distance away because I could see the entire planet through the window, which was about the size of a car windshield. Crote explained to me that we each needed to be put into some kind of sleep/hibernation for ten years. The ten years was important. I started to cry. My daughter was there and she was only sixteen years old. I was only thirty-seven. I didn't want to sleep away all those years of our lives. He then told me that we would not age during that time. He said, "Look" and held a long thin finger to the window. I could see massive explosions happening all over the Earth, left to right, top to bottom. It looked like nuclear war, or possibly massive volcanoes, all happening one right after the other. Crote told me there was no other option, that if we wanted to survive, we had to go to sleep for ten years. We would be returned to the Earth when it was safe. I resignedly went back to my family to explain, and apparently Crote or another alien already had because some of them were asleep, encapsulated in a slim bed-type apparatus with the tube coming out of one nostril, or they were being prepped for that. My mother was arguing, saying she was tired and didn't want to live that long anyway. My sister and I lay down side by side and I could feel the slim tubing glide into my nose.

The next thing I was aware of was being awakened by Crote. I thought there must have been a mistake but he was telling me that the ten years were up. Not everyone had survived—my mom had chosen to leave, and some of the other people were dead. But the rest of my family was okay. Crote told me he had a surprise for me and took me to the cockpit of the ship. There was my daughter, now a full-grown woman, standing at the helm. She turned to smile at me. She had long hair and beautiful teeth (at the time of the dream she had braces on her teeth). I was angry because I had missed out on all the years of her growing up, and turned to Crote. "You promised we wouldn't age!" He told me that my daughter wanted to come out of hibernation early to

38

learn to fly the ship and get to know the aliens better. It had been her choice.

Many years later, sometime after 2005, I came home from work one day to see my daughter standing at the kitchen sink. She turned to smile at me and BAM like lightning it struck me that she was in the pose she had been in that long-ago dream. Her hair was highlighted and long, her braces long gone, and she was even wearing a turquoise shirt just like in the dream. This was one of the triggering moments they had implanted in me, to remember a specific dream at a specific time in my life. I hugged my daughter tearfully, and she was a little confused as to why I was so emotional. All she was doing was standing at the sink doing dishes. I could not begin to explain to her, nor did I even try.

*＊＊＊*

## 1986

*Dreamed I was at an amusement park and some kids were calling me to come into a dark tunnel for a new ride. I was a little nervous but after all, this had to be safe if it was an amusement park. Once I got into the tunnel they closed a door behind me and it was pitch black. There were lots and lots of people, lost souls bumping into each other, warm bodies in the dark. Some were afraid like me, others were evil and I could sense their bad intentions. Someone grabbed me and threw me through a door, then dragged me out onto a swaying suspension bridge. I fell off into the cold water below. I tried to swim through the murky water but it came into my lungs and I drowned. Instead of darkness or fear however, I was suddenly free, freer than I'd ever felt in my life. It was like flying and I knew those evil people would never bother me again.*

*As terrifying as this dream was, I didn't wake up frightened or even feeling bad; in fact I still had that free feeling. Apparently the part of me that drowned or died in that dream was a false sense of self that has been holding me back through guilt, fear, or timidity. —undated; circa late 1980s*

The late 1980s were a time when the aliens and I were still testing each other out, setting boundaries, discovering one another. I do believe this was a turning point in my ability to be less fearful of the dream experiences, and they had a hand in freeing me of these fears by forcing me to fall off that bridge.

*I am alone and three white-haired men carrying briefcases are walking behind me. They won't hurt me but I am afraid to face them. They are from a school or college. I keep walking alone into the mist.*

*Interpretation—I always seem to have someone helping me, yet they are beside me, usually the right side, and slightly to the rear so I can't see them or know who they are, I just feel their presence and aid. There is always at least one but usually two or three. It's funny because sometimes I sense a "presence" at my right side even when awake. —June 7, 1986*

*I was blind, and was aware of being blind, yet I could see, although everything was hazy. I was stumbling around and there was someone helping me. I was on a dock looking for a boat. —June 13, 1986*

*Two or three times during the night I woke up, startled, out of a deep sleep with the knowledge that someone was in the house and coming to get me, maybe kill me. I was really scared. This is like all those old dreams of someone coming after me with a knife to kill me, usually while I'm in bed asleep. A part of me must die to make room for changes. Next time this happens I must stay asleep and face him (her?). —June 13, 1986*

*I was on a sailing yacht with lots of other people and we were laughing and happy and feeling really free, headed for Mexico. It was hot and sunny and beautiful. I was very happy. When we got to Mexico everyone was asleep. I went out on deck to see where we were and it was a bizarre landscape of tufts of mashed potatoes with one or two palm trees growing out of them, sitting in the water. The water was beautiful, clear and calm. —June 21, 1986 (summer solstice)*

In 1986 the visits stepped up in intensity, still extremely fearful, but were now infused with a sense of helpfulness or assistance. This year my first marriage was hitting rock bottom and I was going through a personal emotional transformation. Perhaps the aliens used those emotions and experiences to make a way into my mind and reach me on a new level. Any time our lives go through a transformation— whether it be a move, a shift in relationship status, large losses or gains, financial issues, health concerns—it creates a shift or cracks in our personal reality and thus the aliens can reach us through the cracks. Such was my experience in the summer of 1986 when they were telling me that there was far more to my life than a disintegrating marriage.

\*\*\*

## Time Travel

Part of the work they're doing with us is "adjusting" our future. We have possible futures and probable futures, and working with the aliens helps to determine which future we will experience. They are working to adjust our attitudes and beliefs about our future from one of utter desolation to one of freedom, joy, and abundance for all. Unfortunately, most of us feel rather negatively about our futures or the future of the planet, but they are here to tell us it need not be that way. The scenes of a desolate, post-apocalyptic, zombie-filled future is only a Hollywood story, not the reality we can create. It's not the reality the aliens want for us.

Every once in a while they toss me a dream that causes me to wonder, is there even a message or meaning here? Is this an alien dream or just my addled overly stressed mind creating a nonsense dream? I debated whether or not to include this dream because it doesn't seem to fit in the rest of the messages and yet in a weird way it does. It's possibly been given to me by a different alien than I usually interact with, or it could be a glimpse of our future given that some of my dreams have had prophetic imagery. It could also be a peek at an entirely different culture and world than we know. But because they have often told me that they do not perceive time the same way we do, I decided to include this short dream:

*I lived and worked with a group of people—a black man, a Hispanic woman, a small white dog—and we worked for a delivery service THAT DELIVERS TO DIFFERENT TIMELINES.*

*At the start I was at the Golden Gate Bridge and suddenly thousands of aliens came up and out of the water, a glowing area, right THROUGH the material of the bridge, and flew away. Cars were honking, people screaming and fainting. I stood on the sidelines watching in fascination when I was suddenly yanked through a boxlike square tunnel with the dog behind me, to the Boss' office where he yelled at me for wrong timing.*

*Then I delivered a car to a museum, I arrived sitting in it, a convertible Rolls Royce, delivered before cars were invented.*

*Then together with the others I was caught in a research lab and questioned, barely escaped through the box exit as it was closing up behind the dog, and landed in our apartment in the future, all reds and oranges and metal. My son appeared to tell me he had gotten in trouble at school for time traveling. —June 12, 2010, night of solar eclipse/new moon*

I do not have a son—in this life. The dream has multiple layers of meanings and is unlike anything I have dreamed before or since. I think it was a way of showing me the possibilities are endless, and not to feel blocked in by time constraints or the material world.

*I was at a huge dam and a few of us knew it was about to burst because of some kind of explosions above us (in the sky?). I knew this would be happening to dams all over the world so Mother Earth could rightfully reclaim the waterways that were hers.*

*A group of us were scrambling to climb as high as we could until we were on a grassy area above the dam. I could see many tugboats in the water and something like locks as the water rose on the other side of the dam.*

*When the dam broke the water reached where we were and I saw a tugboat come dangerously close to me and I worried whether it had propellers.*

*The few of us who survived ended up at a building by some glass elevators and we could see the huge belts and cogwheels that operated the elevators. They had something to do with operating time as well.*
*—January 20, 2000*

It's possible the "tugboats" were alien ships because I remember they didn't look like ordinary boats, which is why I was unsure if there was a propeller or not. Glass elevators are a frequent component of my alien dreams. They may be representative of actual ships, because it has been shown to me that their walls can be transformed into perfectly clear walls, appearing much like the fancy glass elevators in nice hotels, or they may be actual elevators into an alternate reality.

*I was in a warehouse made into makeshift barracks with cots amidst the boxes and shelves. We seemed to be just waking up. There was a woman in the cot to my left and a man who looked like John Candy next to her. We had our gear under our cots, and personal photos and posters over our cots. Suddenly it went pitch black. I froze. We saw flashing lights through the high windows. Some people panicked that we were under attack. The auxiliary lights came on and we got orders to get dressed and ready. We dressed together; nothing was sexual because this was too important to mess around with.*

*Then I was at the crash site of a meteor. There was a fire and panicked people. Our job was to control the crowd. Once we got the people out of the way I was taken close to the meteor and shown it was actually a crashed spaceship. They opened it and took out some books and a record. It was a small craft, round, about the size of a VW Beetle.*

Suddenly I was in a vehicle on another planet. It looked like Earth but the sky was darker and the trees were much taller, very thin and tall like the Sequoias. We were following a dirt road and the light was poor. There were odd-looking cars on the road but not many. They kind of looked like old 1950s Cadillacs with the fins.

Somehow the "meteor UFO" came down on this planet too, in a fireball. We went to its landing point and it had landed on the hood of a car but the occupant (tall, thin) wasn't hurt or scared. The person with me opened the craft and gave the car's occupant the books and record inside. Then he (the person with me) turned to me and said, **Your planet is not ready, it would shoot us down and kill us. These people are more primitive than you technologically, but they are not ruled by fear. Perhaps they will use this information to find you.** The occupant was fascinated with the books and the record. —September 21, 2014 (autumnal equinox)

There are multiple layers of meaning to their interactions with us. When they terrify us with visions of nuclear war they're not only trying to shake us awake, but they're also studying our fear reactions. There are many layers; different ways of reaching us physically, mentally, and emotionally. —October 5, 2014

About 1½ hours after falling asleep I woke up screaming. I had heard "them" coming as I fell asleep. There were two beings, one tall and one short. Both were holding swords. The short one had a skinny but long sword, holding it upright. The blades of both swords glowed pure white, almost like the light sabers on Star Wars. The taller being had a wider, taller sword. What made me scream was that the taller one leaned over me, took his sword and very slowly and methodically placed the tip of his sword at the exact point of the scar on my right temple. It was as I felt it penetrating my scalp that I screamed.

I woke up this morning with NO PAIN in my head for the first time in four years. Last night was four years to the day that I had the craniotomy done! —August 28, 2001

*The instrument they did "surgery" on my headache involved a scalpel tip with a handle, all of it glowing metal, pliable. A piece on the bottom waved back and forth to match my vibrational frequency. They "inserted" the scalpel directly inside my skull and brain by intermingling with the atoms by vibrating at the same frequency as my physical body; it slid right in without disturbing my anatomy. It calmed the neurons, the electron firing, stopped the sharp throbbing pain, spread a warmth and "smoothness" over my head. —undated*

It was after the above dreams that it dawned on me—the aliens were here to help me. They knew that I was suffering and had been suffering since my surgery in August 1997, and they sent two people to take away my pain with their white "light sabers" and "scalpel." It was another step for me in learning to trust them more and fear them less.

\*\*\*

*Last night had night terror. I know it was real because I screamed so loud my throat was still hurting when I woke up. So was my broken finger—my left hand and arm are somehow connected with this—the terror was of a cemetery. My husband was absently rubbing my back to calm me down; yet this morning he says there was no dream! And Mom and Dad can't remember the terrors I had as a child. My sister only remembered when I prompted her—this is BIZARRE, FREAKY, SCARY STUFF! Since January 1st I have been having intense night terrors. By May they were every night, including our anniversary on May 7 when I dislocated and fractured my left ring finger. I had one night with three terrors. But why does nobody else remember these? Is there some force keeping them secret? I went to the library to special-order a library book about night terrors that had to come from some university library. They said they would call when it came in but they have not yet called. —July 11, 2002 (7/11/2002 very spiritual numerology)*

*I called the library—they have no record of me asking for the book on night terrors. They have no record of any such book anywhere! — August 2002*

This illustrates one of the most trying, difficult and haunting aspects of these experiences. Not only has my own memory, my own reality, been distorted but it seems that the people close to me also have theirs altered. How is it possible that my parents can't remember my night terrors, can't recall that I ran screaming down the hall like hellfire into their room at least twice a week for the entire time I lived with them? I had a pillow and blanket on the floor next to their bed. How could my sister not recall it? Thank God she did after I brought it to her attention, but it took a little coaxing. And the book, the one I special-ordered from a university library, just disappeared? Along with the request form I filled out for it? It's hard to wrap my head around reality when it shifts and twists like this.

The broken finger I mention happened during another night terror that I had not written in my dream journal—naturally I couldn't because I'm left-handed and my left hand was in a cast for six weeks. It was my husband's and my eight-year wedding anniversary on May 7, 2002, and after a great dinner and celebration, we had gone to sleep. I suddenly awoke, screaming bloody murder, at 1:30 a.m. There was a green monster at the side of my bed pulling on my left arm, trying to pull me out of bed to go somewhere with him. I was terrified, flailing about, and hit my left hand on the wall at the head of the bed, but the monster grabbed my hand and pulled really hard. I screamed again, waking myself up, and he disappeared like mist in the sun. My left hand was hurting really bad. Coming out of the daze I could see the outline of my hand in the dim room and my ring finger was backward. It was pulled out of its socket and was leaning back toward the back of my hand. Instinctively I pulled off my wedding ring, knowing it was going to swell up. I was screaming from pain and shock when my husband finally woke up (this is what makes me feel that the aliens give a little something to the other people in the house when they do an abduction—how is it possible that he didn't hear anything prior to this? And when he did wake up he was groggy). "My hand! My finger!" I screamed. "I broke my finger!"

My husband flipped on the light and stared at my grotesquely distorted finger, which was already turning a pale purple color. "Okay, we're going to the hospital," he said calmly, getting out of bed to dress. He was so used to my nighttime shenanigans that he didn't even ask what happened. On some level, he already knew.

I don't even need to tell you how the hospital staff reacted when we arrived at the ER, me in a robe, holding my left hand up and encased in an ice pack, and telling them that it happened due to a bad dream. The nurses all gave hate stares to my poor supportive husband, obviously believing that he broke my finger. It was dislocated and fractured. They gave me a temporary splint and the next day I went to an orthopedist to have a proper cast placed. He didn't believe the "it was a bad dream" explanation either. I slept on the left side of the bed, and some creature was pulling on my left hand as it hung over the side of the bed. That's all I can say. It was not a friendly creature, and I have not seen it since. It was after this experience that I read that abductions can be stopped by saying, "In the name of Jesus Christ, I demand that you leave," or as I prefer to say, "If you do not come in the name of Jesus Christ, I demand that you leave." This way, if they are the "good guys" they are welcome to come, because I know that the good ones have provided healing for me, comfort and reassurance. If they were here to kill me or eat me or whatever, they could have and would have done so long ago. I know in my heart that they are here to help us heal the Earth, to repair what we have damaged, and they come in the spirit of helpfulness and Love. And Love is what Jesus is all about.

*My husband said that last night I sat up in bed and had a conversation with someone who wasn't there. I was saying, "How am I going to do that?" and "I can't see, it's dark." He said I didn't scream this time. Wow, maybe my instincts have been right all along, that this experience is real and they are talking to me for real. —July 26, 2002*

*I was at a large spooky house, watching three foster kids. They were good kids, quiet, but had oddly big heads and one of them was completely bald. When I had to use the bathroom the older girl followed me in and sat on a child's potty, then asked me how to use toilet paper. She seemed to be about 7 or 8 years old and I thought it was odd that she didn't know how to use TP. I showed her how to tear the pieces off the roll when another lady came to stand in the doorway and said, "Only use two squares, otherwise you're wasting it." My mom used to tell me that and this lady made me angry. I told the girl she can use as much TP as she needs to use. She copied my technique as I wiped, which made me a little uncomfortable.*

*We returned to the main room of the house, where a man who looked like actor Scott Wolf asked me to go with him and take the kids to a better place. He was doing something with the aliens where they were planning and designing houses. While the aliens were looking at the blueprints, we sneaked away with the kids to a small airplane, which Scott said he could fly. We got away but then a huge round airplane flew over us and landed on top of our plane with a loud CLANG. It was stuck to us as though with a strong magnet. —November 17, 2014*

It's interesting that although I had no problem with Scott Wolf working with aliens, I was surprised that we were overtaken by an obvious UFO. I believe the "foster kids" were, in reality, hybrid children, a mixture of alien and human DNA. The aliens don't have elimination systems so this would completely explain their fascination with our bathrooms and use of toilet paper—and their children's utter lack of knowledge about such things.

*They are letting me see them more and more, and I have not screamed for a couple weeks now. I think I am learning to conquer the fear at the same time they are learning how not to scare me.*

*Lights don't scare me anymore. Last night I woke up to something (an instrument) being put down my throat; like the night before they were doing something medically to my chest, something to do with my heart. This time it made me cough and I woke up, and they showed me the brilliant lime-green light floating, about 6 inches long by 4 inches wide, shaped weird. It was metal even though it glowed a brilliant lime green. I was not afraid!! —September 11, 2002*

\*\*\*

# Chapter 3

## Aliens

Naturally there are many different alien species. Looking at all the known living species here on Earth, from the depths of the oceans to mountaintops to geothermal extremes, from microscopic life to the giant whales, it's natural for all life to be varied and unusual. Why wouldn't that continue out into the reaches of space?

For the longest time, whenever I asked the aliens who they were or where they came from they would reply, ***Names are not important. The message is what is important.*** Impersonal, cold, aloof. But names were important to me! It would somehow make them less frightening to know they had names, lives, families, maybe even pets; to know that they did not exist solely to terrify me.

As years passed and various aliens approached me, I came to understand some of their differences. It is the Greys who act indifferent and robotic, and I have yet to know a name for any of them individually. Others, however, have come to trust me in the way that I have come to trust them and we share a friendship, dare I say a bond or even affection. We have found a common ground in our love for Mother Earth and I have proven to them that I am of good intent and will not willfully hurt any of them; they in turn have lessened the fearful way in which they approach me and they no longer perform scary medical experiments on me. In fact, if I am experiencing any kind of pain, whether physical or emotional, related to them or not, they will come and help alleviate it.

As we came to trust one another, they individually began telling me their names and a little bit about themselves. I think they finally realized that this helps to lessen the anxiety that their contact generates in humans if they let us know who they are, where they are from, and what they are up to. These are the aliens who have let their guard down enough to introduce themselves to me over the years.

\*\*\*

## Kyiesos

Kyiesos (Kie-EE-sos) is not male nor female but androgynous. Kyiesos appears cat-like or monkey-like, is of plant-based origin, and is very connected to the Earth and all its living creatures, plant and animal; humans less often. It is difficult for her to be around humans as they can be extremely negative and destructive and violent. I refer to this person as "she" because there is a female, nurturing energy about it and I really dislike referring to such a loving gentle being as "it," although this entity is clearly neither male nor female and there is no visible genitalia.

Kyiesos introduced herself to me in 2005 shortly after my beautiful dog Kandee died. *She has Kandee*, I wrote, encased in a heart— *undated*. I was grieving the loss of this incredibly smart, sensitive, psychic animal who was part golden retriever, part border collie, and all love. She traumatically died in my husband's arms early one summer morning. Knowing she moved on to the realm where Kyiesos lives makes her loss easier for me to bear.

The drawing to the left is the first time Kyiesos made herself directly known to me. I wrote: *Last night I went to bed with smoky quartz crystal (under pillow, because the night before I slept with green calcite in my hand and something happened in the night; I woke up and the green calcite was smashed on the floor in my office). I "woke up" ½ hour after going to bed to see the creature Kyiesos (cat-like) staring at me from next to the bed, like Kandee used to do. As soon as I saw Kyiesos, "it" floated up and disappeared, jetted away up and to my right. I saw a brown tail, monkey-like but the rest of it looked very cat-like. —August 20, 2005*

I went on to describe tufted brown fuzzy hair on Kyiesos's head; pointy feet that wavered in the air as though it was treading water; whiskers or antennae on either side of the puckery mouth; pointed ears on either side of the head; and arms that outstretched to show wings somewhat like those of a flying squirrel.

I went to bed with a crystal under my pillow that night because crystals aid my dreaming abilities, especially the ability to remember them. They also calm and relax me with their gentle vibration. The night of August 19 I had gone to bed with a small green calcite in my hand. I was having trouble sleeping because my husband and I had recently separated. When I awoke the next morning I found the green calcite smashed into many pieces on the tile floor of my office (which was across the hall from my bedroom), with pieces extending out into the hall as if the crystal had been thrown with great force. I had no recall of anything happening that night. So the next night I used my large smoky quartz crystal and placed it safely under my pillow.

On the opposite side of the above paper I had written @ *menopause > sacred wisdom keeper.* I was upon the threshold of menopause and feeling ambivalent about it, a sense of loss, loss of womanliness, loss of fertility, loss of attractiveness. But Kyiesos encouraged me to know that nothing is a loss without some form of gain, the gain for menopausal losses being wisdom; the wisdom of having lived enough years, survived enough experiences, to share with others and assist younger women through their travails. I never had a grandmother and was not especially close with my own mother, so I could now make up for those losses by being a maternal wisdom keeper, a type of grandmother, for other young women.

Kyiesos is very concerned with the healing not only of our planet but also of the women on our planet and the place of women in our society. I believe she is from the future, as I wrote:

*Gleanings from Kyiesos of the future:*

*PASSION*

*Have you lost your passion?*

*FIBROMYALGIA*

*Mostly occurs in women who are empathetic, compassionate. Related to Mother Earth. Points of pain resonate with "points of pain" i.e. areas of conflict on Mother Earth. Keep a journal, listen to the body, pay attention to the weather.*

*Men are more connected with Father Sky—more distant and far-reaching.*

## BLADDER

*Bladder issues are more common in humans who incarnated from planets where the beings did not have bladders/gastrointestinal systems. So when we incarnate on this planet we have a hard time with them. Bladder issues can also mean you are PISSED OFF!*

## SIMPLIFY

*Eat as if you lived in the garden. No diets.*

## ELIMINATE SHOULD

*Using the word "should" leads to apathy. "I should be working somewhere else. I should be thinner. I should live differently." These lead to apathy. Please eliminate this word from your vocabulary. If you must, replace it with "as if." "I will act as if I work somewhere else. I will eat as if I am thinner. I will live as if things were different." Acting "as if" will help to bring the desired changes about; it will enact change rather than the passive "should." —October 28, no year, sometime after 2005*

Whereas the other aliens are evasive about telling me about themselves, Kyiesos is quite direct. **I am Kyiesos of the future**, she tells me. I am then shown a quick series of images conveying that she is a plant-based person surviving on photosynthesis rather than eating food and that her native habitat is a thick, lush green jungle. *Most advanced lifeforms are breatharians, obtaining their nutrients from their air; or they evolved from plant life and obtain nutrition from photosynthesis. —March 2014*

I first saw Kyiesos in 1986 while living in a big home with my first husband. We had a lovely large split-leaf philodendron which had been given to us as a wedding gift from a dear friend in 1978. Eight years later it had grown into a five-foot-tall glorious plant that I kept in our bright, sunny bedroom. One night I awakened from a bad dream (back in 1986 these experiences were still only "bad dreams" to me, though deep down I knew better) and lay in bed, gasping for breath, when I gazed over at the philodendron shimmering in the moonlight. There was a distinctly feminine face rising out of the leaves; it reminded me of the wooden women carved as figureheads of old wooden sailing ships, the way the body rose from the base of the plant itself; two smaller leaves looked like arms and hands, and a larger, newly unfurling leaf, created the face. It had a serene expression, peaceful. When its eyes turned to me there was a lingering moment of recognition before she disappeared from view and all that was there was the plant, my split-leaf philodendron (*Monstera deliciosa*). Delicious monster. Now why did anyone give a plant that name? Whose face was living in my plant?

It was not until 2005 that I was formally introduced to Kyiesos, but I feel she has been near me most of the time. I love plants, always have, and worked with plant nurseries and landscaping for years. Whenever I am upset, feeling ill, tired, frustrated, or negative in any way, I work with plants and feel a great sense of peace and healing.

She is quite audibly present and gives great verbal information, and I can sense her presence, but visually she is not as clear as some of the others. When I do catch sight of her she is very graceful, like a palm tree swaying in the wind, even when there is no wind. She has large eyes and a small mouth, and no nose at all. Being a plant person, she uses photosynthesis for nutrients and respiration and therefore has no need of a nose. Technically I wonder why she has a mouth either, as she communicates telepathically, but I seem to be on a need-to-know basis with the alien people and they are the ones who ask the questions, not me. Sure I can ask all I want, but I don't often get answers.

\*\*\*

## Watchers

*I opened a file called EARTH 12-18-57A. It was a Life Review. I kept seeing a small purple entity above me and to my left, it was circular and had long tentacles like a jellyfish. It had 2 antennae on top. The bright purple lights would glow suddenly, become tracers almost like fireworks, then fade away. Then it would begin again. It was either me, my higher self, or a WATCHER.*

*I was in a theater with lots of people watching a group review. Dogs and cats were there too, living and dead. We saw flashes of magazine covers, ones that had happened and ones that had never happened, to review our time on Earth. We were reviewing what had happened, and making a consensus decision on what is to come ...*

*I also saw files:*

> *Earth 12-18-57B*
>
> *Earth 12-18-57C*
>
> *_____12-18-57A*
>
> *_____ 12-18-57B*

*but I am forbidden to remember the names on the last two files, or the contents of any of them. Apparently the life I am living now is 12-18-57A. —undated*

My birthday is 12-18-1957 so it seemed like an assortment of possible futures and probable futures but, regardless, I was destined to be born on that date. The last two must have been the names of other planets and I am forbidden to recall that information. I do not know what a WATCHER is but seemed to know at the time of this writing.

***

## Ahtehkanah

Pronounced just as it's spelled—Ah Teh Ka Nah—This is a sweet and gentle spirit that allows herself to be seen easily. The first time I sketched her picture was in January of 2003 after a disturbing dream. She was there to comfort me.

*Dream early this morning—was in an apartment and had a large-screen TV and a smaller one. Was cleaning up, had the three dogs with me, when I heard a deep, pulsating throbbing hum and all the power suddenly went out. Everything was bathed in a reddish-orange glow. I looked at the big-screen TV, which flashed some type of message to me before going off. It triggered me to remember something and I said aloud, "This is just like my dream!" Then something pulled on my leg and I felt very heavy. I laid down on the ground, the dogs were also down. It was like gravity had increased. It was déjà vu, a dream within a dream. When it ended I got up, the dogs were fine, and I went outside. All the neighbors were outside—all races and ages—and an Asian man and his father were talking to me in a foreign language. —January 31, 2003*

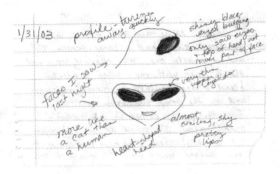

This is a picture of the "Asian man" in my dream. Years later I learned it was a female alien. This shows how a screen memory works—how could I have been talking to these beings and thought they were just regular people?

It was four years before I drew her again, but that doesn't mean I didn't see her many times in between. Often the dreams are so foggy upon waking that I can remember parts but not enough to sketch or even write.

Ahtehkanah officially introduced herself to me in July 2007. She is a slightly different type of alien, as mentioned above, almost angelic; wispy, soft, gentle. Her specialty must be that of healing, both of mind and body. She has extremely long arms and fingers with a gentle touch and no temperature; neither hot nor cold. She is pure white in appearance with a lovely heart-shaped mouth. However, when she smiled she had a huge row of sharp pointy shark-like teeth which made me gasp. When she realized the teeth scared me, she kept her mouth closed and continues now to smile with it closed.

There was a period in July 2007 where she visited me every night. Unfortunately, I can't remember what exactly was going on in my personal life at that time, but I'm sure I was upset about something because she is a great comforter. In the description I write: *Wispy, translucent but with penetrating eyes. EXTREME GENTLENESS. —July 16, 2007.* A couple of months later I added an excerpt: *She came to me again this morning when I had a severe headache. She has a heart-shaped face. This is where our mythology of a heart shape comes from ...*

By "wispy, translucent," I meant her form was ghostlike and frail. From both of the sketches she appears to have no type of profile, or none that I could glean. She is a healer or comforter, coming to me when I am in intense pain, particularly with migraine headaches, which I suffer from frequently. A recurring cycle of migraines could be the reason she was "stopping by" frequently during that particular July.

It was the next morning that she arrived and let me know her name. I again awoke in the early morning hours with an extremely bad migraine headache and she appeared to me. She didn't tell me directly, but I knew telepathically that her name was Ahtehkanah.

*Woke up with horrible migraine, have been fighting it since yesterday. Woke up at 5 a.m. and this creature was sitting on my bed.* [She smiled at me showed large sharp shark-like pointy teeth which made me gasp in shock and surprise. Was she going to eat me? Those looked like carnivorous teeth! As soon as she realized it scared me, she smiled with her mouth shut. From now on whenever I see her, she keeps her heart-shaped mouth closed!] *She put her hands on my forehead and alleviated pain > in thanks I asked her to lay down and spoon with me > she was afraid to relax and let go so near a human but I gently held her for a moment, then like a wispy cloud on a summer breeze she slipped out of my grasp— but not before I could tell her that there are advantages to having a human body—or for that matter, an earthly body. —July 17, 2007 (Fire the Grid Day)*

I could not see the lower half of her body so do not know what kind of feet or fins she might have. She was pure white but translucent. She emanated such unconditional love, gentleness, and sense of healing that I felt the desire to hold her close. She is timid, especially of humans, though she loves us deeply.

*She* [Ahtehkanah] *came to me again this morning when I had a severe headache. She has a heart-shaped face. I believe this is where the heart shape of our mythology comes from. —September 27, 2007 (9-9-9 in numerology).*

The hearts that beat in our chests look nothing like the heart shape used for Valentine's Day. Her face, however, and her lips, have that heart shape. She is so full of gentleness, compassion, and love that it is no wonder that shape has come to be the representation of love in our culture.

*Many in your part of the world are having difficulty producing offspring. Why? There are many reasons, not the least of which is the chronic poisoning of your environment which of course affects the physical body.*

*PASSION means uniting in intimacy of body, spirit, mind, and emotions. Sex is not just for breeding purposes, it is to unify with passion. Note the word procreation; pro-creation. Creating life.* — *undated*

She then told me how passion relates to creation of new life, and how couples who are infertile sometimes lose their passion by concentrating on time schedules, temperatures, medication dosages. Sometimes a couple cannot conceive and if they break up or one of them has an affair, a conception can suddenly happen because passion has been ignited with someone new. Certainly that isn't considered to be an option for those who are struggling with fertility, but I was told to put out a reminder that passion is a very important and often overlooked aspect of fertility. Many indigenous peoples understood that, having rites of passage, special fertility ceremonies that sometimes lasted for days, getting everyone in the tribe inspired and impassioned. It is a reminder to step back, stop the worry and stress for a month or so, and re-ignite the passion you originally felt when love was new and life was full of possibilities. Ahtehkanah is quite concerned with human health and happiness, and wishes joy and passion for all.

\*\*\*

## The Greys

No discussion of alien lifeforms would be complete without mentioning the Greys. There have been numerous books, theories, webpages, and stories about them but I will just stick with my own personal experience and let the reader decide. Take what rings true for you and discard the rest.

When Whitley Strieber came out with his book *Communion* in 1987 I saw this cover in a bookstore window and was immediately frozen to the spot.1 I was terrified. I was entranced. I was mesmerized. Up until the moment I saw this picture I had believed my scary dreams were just that—scary, albeit highly realistic, dreams. Now here was a total stranger who not only had scary dreams like mine, but the faces, oh my God the faces …

It wasn't quite right though.

I kept staring. Those eyes, oh yes, the eyes were right. But my alien's faces had either no nose or a nose that only consisted of two tiny round nostrils flat on the face. And the mouth wasn't right; the mouth of my creatures was puckery and roundish, almost like an anus. The chin on this picture was too pointy. And the skin of my creatures was exactly like dolphin skin, the same color, the same texture. At that time I didn't know how I knew what their texture was, but yet I did. Dolphins. Years later I touched a dolphin with a sense of wonder and fascination. My Greys have dolphin skin. But those eyes … they were dead on.

Book cover from COMMUNION: A TRUE STORY by WHITLEY
STRIEBER. COPYRIGHT © 1987 BY WILSON AND NEFF, INC. Reprinted
by permission of HarperCollins Publishers.

The Greys with whom I have interacted over the years have been
at my side, literally. They are the helper guides for the other aliens.
They are the ones who wake me up, get me out of bed, and guide me to

wherever we are going. There are almost always three of them; one at each side and one behind me. The ones at my side stay slightly behind me so that I can sense their presence but not watch them—they watch me instead. Most often they guide me by holding onto my upper arms with their small frog-like hands. Three fingers and a thumb, with something like suction cups at the tips of the fingers. If I struggle or fight with them, I awaken with bruises on my upper arms but they don't intentionally hurt me. They are in reality very timid and gentle, and actually are afraid of the brute strength and horrifying brutality of human beings.

As far as I can tell they do not wear clothing and if that's the case, they don't seem to have genitalia, though I have had the sense of some of them being distinctly either male or female. If they do wear clothing it is very form-fitting like some kind of leotard, but as I said above they feel like a dolphin so I don't know what kind of fabric that would be. Alien fabric I suppose!

They don't have feet. They have flippers at the end of their legs and they do not walk, rather they float or glide through our atmosphere the way we glide through water while swimming or treading water. They are about three feet tall, though they vary in size and color just as humans do.

They are the assistants, the helpers. They work with the other aliens to carry out menial tasks. They are not as sensitive as the others and seem unaware or uncaring if I am frightened or hurting. I don't believe this means they are evil; they simply don't understand human emotions. They are like ants or worker bees, carrying out their duties simply and without drama. This is their job. I have seen other alien types who don't interact with humans but assist with flying a ship or doing cleanup work, but the Greys are in direct contact with humans. They set up the exam rooms and assist with examinations. I've read theories that they are robotic, but I believe that they are living beings; they simply exist on an entirely different wavelength than we do, making communication and interaction extremely difficult. On occasion one or two have tried to communicate with me, as curious about me as I am about them,

but the communication is quite limited. Some have listened intently as I communicate with Crote or others. They are learning and evolving through these experiences just as I am.

*The rocks in the water don't know how the rocks in the sun feel.* ~ *Haitian proverb*

*The greys are intermediaries. Amphibians, they can live in both worlds. We are the fish. Mantids are the shore birds. Greys know BOTH WORLDS. —undated*

\*\*\*

## Flying Greys?

I have an undated sketch of what appears to be a Grey with wings. It has the profile of Ahtehkanah, has filmy translucent wings like the fairy beings, and those funny finlike feet and suction-cup tree frog fingers, which many of my alien friends seem to have. The head is very much like a Grey, and I recall the size of the entity being similar to that of a five-year-old child.

Along with the entity I drew its shiny silver instrument, further causing me to believe it's a Grey since they usually do the medical procedures or assist with them. This instrument resembles one that has been put up my nose in the past; long, shiny, with some kind of bulb at the end.

I noted that the *Egyptians molded their heads to look like that* [the ancient Mayans did as well], *and the Chinese bound their feet to look like that. Frog-like head with a puckery mouth (almost like an anus!), no neck and no shoulders. The filmy translucent "wings?" can disappear or fold in; bat-like in shape but translucent like a dragonfly. —undated*

They appear to work in the same capacity of the nonflying Greys. Who knows, maybe all Greys can fly but they simply fold in their wings at times to make them nonperceptible. These flying Greys may look almost demonic to people, but I assure you they are not. Before I accepted that the aliens are benevolent and helpful I went through a phase where someone told me they were demons. I do believe in our one Creator, and I have a personal relationship with Jesus, but I was unsure about the whole concept of demons. I attended Unity Church, which teaches that there are no demons, only negativity on the part of human thinking. Looking around the world, listening to the news, one cannot help but believe there is some intense negativity infecting this planet. I woke up with such extreme terror after being in contact with the aliens that I just had to be sure they were not evil. For about two years, whenever I sensed alien beings, or even if I was lucid enough to do it during an actual abduction, I would say three times: "If you come in the name of Jesus Christ, I welcome you. If you do not come in the name of Jesus Christ, I demand that you leave." There was only one instance in which I felt a withdrawal of energies around me, and I assume that had been a negative-based alien. After that, I felt freer, lighter, happier, and far less afraid of the experiences. That is when the aliens started to tell me their names and interact on a more personal level with me, and allow me fuller recall of our encounters. Therefore, there likely are negative aliens, just as there are negative humans, but the majority of aliens, and certainly all the ones I work with, are positive and want the best and highest outcome for the good of all involved.

***

## Alien Pets?

While I've observed and interacted with several different types of aliens I've seen at least two types who cause me to wonder if they are pets or some type of companion animals (companion aliens?).

The first type I've seen being carried by Greys and others when they are not running around on the ground. They are small, dark brown, and furry. They move very fast and, when not being carried, can only be seen scurrying quickly from my peripheral vision. If I try to look at them straight on I cannot see them; I can only glimpse them through the corners of my eyes. They are low to the ground, speeding around. Although they move fast, they lope along kind of like a bear, like a sped-up video of a bear lumbering along. They appear to have four legs, no tail, and I have not seen a face or snout; they almost seem to have body and head all as one atop four legs. They are about the size of a cocker spaniel or a large, fat cat. They are so quick and fleeting that I have very little information about them, but I've seen them aboard every ship I've been on and have often seen them scampering around my home when the aliens come visiting. My own dogs and cats have simply ignored them, as they have with all alien lifeforms.

I've been told that *they clean up messes*. And, as with most things told me by the aliens, this is loaded with multiple layers of meanings. They literally clean up spilled things, because even aliens make mistakes and knock things over, and humans can and do make messes aboard the ships. But these creatures are also capable of moving so fast that they can rearrange our known reality before it happens. If a human sees something they shouldn't, somehow these little brown critters move fast enough to remove that memory from the human before it's recorded in the human's brain and make the event as if it never happened.

Despite their "job description" I have the distinct impression that they are kept as pets by the aliens. I have also seen many regular-looking cats on board ships. I know some abductees bring their cats with them but I do wonder if regular Earth cats aren't kept by aliens as pets as well.

*** 

The other "pet" is more fascinating. I've seen several of them at various times over the years and made sketches, and did not realize until I started assembling notes for this book that they are similar. They're probably not the same entity but from the same species, which, interestingly, look like fairies to me. Could this be the origin of faery stories? They are tiny, maybe a foot tall at the most, with iridescent dragonfly-type wings that are constantly moving. They do not have feet as we do, but rather fin-type feet as they "swim" through our air. They are pastel colored, ranging from pink to aqua to shimmering pale green or blue; every part of them from wings to face to hair. Since they do not appear to be working as the others do, I assume they are companions to the aliens, though of course it's possible that they do have jobs, just not a type of job that I would recognize.

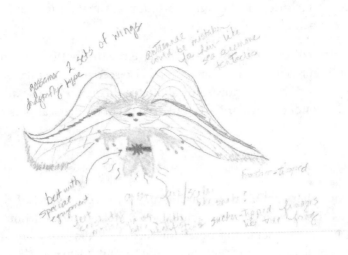

This drawing is not dated but it is fairly recent, circa 2010. As the aliens have come to trust me more, they allow me to see them more vividly. The comments written here are: *Gossamer dragonfly type 2 sets of wings. Antennae could be mistaken for hair—like sea anemone tentacles. Belt with special equipment. Feet constantly moving, waving back & forth like fish fins. Green fur/scales like snake? Sucker-tipped fingers like tree frog. Feather-tipped wings. —undated*

This being was very small, perhaps six inches in height. It is remarkably similar to another drawing I made in the 1970s, circa 1975. I can tell that date as I drew it on the back of a receipt from a cash register where I was working as a cashier for a building supply company in 1975. I had written simply *Alana* at the top, and at that time I was a teenager and thought it was something I had seen in a dream.

The primary difference between these two beings seems to be the pointed head on the earlier one; but as described above the creature had tentacles or antennae on the top, which could seem like hair, and may, in Alana below, have been the same type of antennae, simply upswept somehow.

I had paperclipped the drawing of *Alana* to a short story I had begun writing. I know I was a teenager at the time because of my handwriting. This also shows that I did not believe these experiences were real, but they did make good fodder for a short story in my opinion at that time. I had begun a short story about a character named Jennie who believed she was dying.

*Suddenly out of nowhere came a blinding flash of light, then a strange musical sound, almost like a little song. Then, as Jennie looked up, she saw a tiny little person floating in the air above her. The little creature had big, pale blue wings that gently fluttered in the air. She looked almost like a butterfly, Jennie thought.*

*The musical sound came again, then the creature started to speak. Her voice was very soft and sounded strangely like music. "Come now, Jennie, you've been so brave up to now. You haven't even thought about dying. Why now?"*

*"Who are you?" Jennie somehow found her voice.*

*"I am called Alana. I know you; I know everything about you."*

*"You mean like a guardian angel?" Jennie exclaimed. Then suddenly she became afraid. What on earth was going on?*

The tiny Alana laughed, and it sounded like bells tinkling from far away. "No, not an angel I'm afraid. Just a good friend. Would you like to come with me?"

"Where?"

"To the most fantastic place you've ever dreamed of. I can't even begin to explain it to you, you must see it for yourself."

For all I know these beings are not aliens at all but some kind of fairy or spirit being. But since the very meaning of "alien" is strange or foreign, I chose to include them with the other aliens. For one thing, they all have huge penetrating eyes in common, and to the best of my knowledge all the beings I interact with are some kind of otherworldly/other-dimensional aliens.

A similar being interacted with me in June 2005 and I sketched her upon waking up, then went on to describe the experience. *I woke up, turned to the wall, and saw a fairy—a REAL fairy, lying on her side, floating in the air watching me. She had a tiny, delicate body, golden blonde hair, and a very mature pixie face, big piercing eyes. When she realized I was staring at her she was startled. I blanked out for a moment, then she <u>disappeared</u> in front of my eyes. She stood up in the air and looked like she was doing something, like she was opening a door, then just <u>disappeared</u>. When she realized I could see her, her face had a look of panic. That's when I blanked out. It took me a minute to realize this was all REAL. I looked at my clock—exactly 12:00 midnight. I tried to call her back—could sense her presence—but she was wary of me and wouldn't come back. —June 10, 2005*

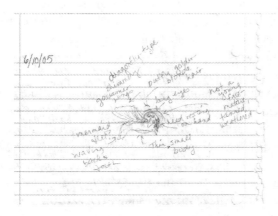

I included in the above picture descriptions eerily similar to the other two; *dragonfly-type shimmery gossamer wings, big eyes, mermaid feet waving back and forth, thin small body.* This one I described with *puffy golden blonde hair and with a mature, tanned, weathered face.*

With this last one in 2005, I was beginning to accept these experiences as real and not dreams after all.

***

## Crote

I saved the best for last. Crote is my closest alien friend. The others come and go fleetingly; the Greys are ever-present but without much personality; but Crote has always been near me. I was eight years old when I had my first clear interaction with him. I awoke after a "bad dream" to a seven-foot-tall praying mantis-type creature standing at the foot of my bed. He was dressed in a cream-colored robe tied at his middle (can't really say he has a waist!) with a fancy rope. There was a high neck on the robe, above which his huge head and black shiny eyes stared down at me. I remember being too terrified to move or scream— or more likely, I had been purposefully paralyzed for his visit. During this visit there were two or three Greys at my head, and one of the creatures spoke to me telepathically, describing a procedure they were going to perform on me. Crote took a long silver wand, about sixteen inches long and very thin, and he spread my legs apart and inserted it into my vagina right there on my bed. I was eight years old! I didn't even know I *had* a vagina! It didn't hurt and was quick but did give me some unfamiliar sexual feelings. So my first sexual feelings were in relation to a giant insect; perhaps that's why I have struggled with relationships in my lifetime? I have come to believe he was harvesting eggs from me; although I had not yet reached puberty the eggs are intact in a female human's ovaries from the time she is born. They are not ripe until puberty, but I believe the aliens have the capabilities to work with unripe human eggs. This harvesting procedure was performed on me multiple times in my life but stopped abruptly after I had surgery to remove my ovaries. I was worried that Crote would stop visiting after that, but he did not. He does visit less frequently however.

My relationship with Crote goes extensively beyond the harvesting of my eggs. He is the one who has been my tour guide on numerous ships. He has been the one to answer most of my questions, foolish or simplistic or not. He has been the one to come to my side when I am in deep pain, whether physical or emotional, and with a simple flourish on my forehead, he removes it instantaneously.

Unlike most of my alien friends who appear not to have feet, Crote has large and powerful hind legs like a hairless kangaroo.

I have been unable to draw Crote with my crude, amateurish sketches. He is so regal, so stately; he carries himself with such grace, that I cannot begin to portray his true characteristics.

It took decades for me to trust him. He did not tell me his name until 2006.

*Just before falling asleep, was visited by "Crote"– an insect-looking person. Very friendly, and chatty like a long-lost friend, completely belying his creepy looks. He had a face like a mole cricket* [but he stood upright on his powerful hind legs].

Mole Cricket

*He told me the mole cricket I saw today at work was really him, observing me. I couldn't make eye contact; he was so creepy. He made me look closely into his eyes and I saw kindness deep down; a sweet, affectionate feeling. I told him that people want to kill mole crickets. He replied,* **No greater love hath one than he who would lay down his life for another.** [A paraphrase of John 15:13 in the Bible: "Greater love hath no man than this, that a man lay down his life for his friends." KJV] *He said it with such compassion, such conviction, I could not help but love him.*

*Then he told me that his people were preparing underground tunnels leading to caves, where some of us would go when "It" happens. I said I had visions of government officials and others going underground and drowning when those areas were flooded. He didn't directly tell me, but implied telepathically that was how they were going to get out of their treaty with the American government (and we know from past history how the American government honors its treaties)—by leading government officials to specific "safe" areas where they would eventually drown. Crote's representatives accompanying them were going to drown for the greater good. Others of us were going to be taken to safe areas. We are being prepared by our dreams and visions, and must trust our inner guidance at all times, even if we are scared. When we are scared we need to take LOVE from the ULTIMATE SOURCE* [God, Divine Mind, Universal Intelligence] *in through the top of our heads and project it out of our chests. Either project to loved ones, to specific locales on planet Earth,*

73

*andomly everywhere. This will protect both projector*
*ctee, exponentially increased, the more people who do*
*it. This is how Crote's people have protected certain locales and*
*humans thus far.*

*As he talked I felt such enormous love for him, but his ap-*
*pearance still creeped me out. He could read my thoughts and*
*feelings, and asked if it was his face, his eyes. I said no, it was*
*all those legs, 6 of them spontaneously waving about. He stood*
*up full length, came towards me and hugged me with all of them,*
*saying, The better to hug you with, my dear. His antennae were*
*tickling my hair. He is able to change size and went from eye lev-*
*el at the edge of my bed* [about 3 feet tall] *to being slightly taller*
*than me at over 5 feet. I got the impression he is naturally about*
*9 to 10 feet tall. —January 10, 2006*

This experience not only did not creep me out, but it intensified
the level of love I felt for Crote. When I was very young my favorite
bedtime story was *Little Red Riding Hood*. He obviously knew that
from having scanned my mind, and knew to use that as a method to
defuse my fear and even invoke a sense of humor about the situation,
reminiscent of the wolf, disguised as Red's grandma, saying such things
as "The better to see you with, my dear."

After Crote said, **The better to hug you with, my dear**, and
stepped forward to hug me with all six of those squirmy, wriggly, creepy
insectoid poky legs, my first instinct was to step back and scream, but
he absolutely engulfed me with that hug. It was so much more than a
physical hug. It was a complete embrace of body, mind, and spirit. It's
what I imagine it feels like to be hugged by an angel. There was such
an incredibly deep sense of unconditional love, acceptance, maternal/
paternal pride, relief, joy, peace; we just don't have the words in our
English vocabulary to describe the completeness and fullness of this
experience. I love many people, have loved and been loved in my
lifetime, and I like to think I am capable of things like unconditional
love, pure love, love without attachments, but I realized in that moment
that human love falls sadly short of true unconditional Love. We will

always have our petty jealousies and fears and worries and insecurities that place a division in our love between ourselves and another. But during that moment (or was it an hour? It was timeless) I shared with Crote I felt the purest, most unconditional form of love that I have ever known. It is real. It is possible. I know it, I have experienced it. This is how they have become more advanced beings than us. They somehow escaped or evolved into higher Love and away from derogatory experiences like the Seven Deadly sins of lust, greed, sloth, gluttony, wrath, envy, and pride. Yet I find it ironic that those are some of the very things they are eager to experience through us, or to study about us. Maybe they feel that they lost something when they lost those emotions. Surely I know that humans are intriguing to them, and that they love us beyond measure. They love us more than we love ourselves because they are capable of a depth of purely positive emotion that we are not.

This was a breakthrough because it was the first time an alien used any type of humor (as I understand humor) to interact with me. They are not especially funny entities in our world. They don't have much of a sense of humor that I've seen; maybe that's just because their humor is on a whole different level than ours, because I do believe that all intelligent life has a sense of humor. Even our pets do silly things to make us laugh. In this interaction with Crote he used the words *The better to hug you with, my dear* as a way to offset my squeamish fear, and we both realized that his attempt at Earth humor threw me off balance just enough that he was able to lean in for that hug. It was a huge new awareness for both of us, and since then I have seen their crude attempts at humor as a way to lighten my fear—for example, peeking around the corner at me from inside the bedroom closet rather than simply awakening me to a brutal stare two inches from my face.

This was the start of a whole new depth to our relationship. I loved Crote. I no longer feared him. How could I? I had experienced his true self, and he had experienced mine. I trusted him completely now. He had used both humor and love to defuse my abject terror, and it worked. This was in 2006, and I like to think it earmarked a new time of alien visitation, as now Crote knew a better way to approach humans without terrifying them. It was a whole new beginning for me and, I like to think, for all interaction between aliens and humans.

Up until that time I had believed that Crote was some type of praying mantis, probably because he stands on his hind legs and is a shiny green-gray color. But after the above communication there was no doubt he was more of a mole cricket. Naturally since both mantids and mole crickets are earthly creatures, Crote is neither one but this is the closest example that my human mind can grasp for comparison. Sometimes he wears a floor-length cream-colored flowing robe tied at the "waist" with a type of rope. It has a hood and looks very similar to the robes worn by the monks of the old world. The hood can be worn up or down, and there is a stiff collar that can be worn up or down, with either one of these partially obscuring his face if he desires.

*About four months ago Crote came to me and told me he had to go away for awhile—I could sense it was important, he had to do important work. I begged him to take me with him but I knew I also have important work here. He reminded me that we belong to each other no matter where/when we are in the universe. He showed me a diamond, a huge multifaceted shimmering diamond, and each facet of the diamond (dozens of them) were an individual expression of his soul. Many I could not see but one facet was him, Crote. One facet was me, Donna. One facet was my second husband; it's one reason why I can't let him go completely, he is literally a part of my soul group.*

*So last night, being the end of the Mayan calendar according to Carl Calleman, I prepared for bed with an onyx dragon's eye crystal under my pillow, wearing my dolphin crystal and a medicine bag with lavender, sage, my lemurian crystal, an Atlantic pearl, a Pacific pearl, and my Larimar Atlantis crystal. I normally don't go to such lengths but have had dark, troubling dreams since Crote left. No bruises on awakening, but can't remember much of the dreams.*

Praying Mantis

*The crystals helped because last night I slept well, had AMAZING dream that I recall from early morning—I was getting ready for graduation. I was in a special Army and me and my Army buddies had special uniforms for graduation. We wore hats like Indiana Jones, special boots, jeans, and a vest with lots of special pockets. I was very proud to be in this Army. My mom, dad, and sister were helping me and kept taking pictures of me that I could see on a giant TV screen. The other Army friends took off for their individual positions. There was a long line to follow to get the diploma and I was nervous. When I started walking I saw a woman I knew who had a huge feather on top of her head. I said, "You have known me since I was a very tiny little girl!" she just smiled knowingly and said,* **I know.** *She held my hand very tightly and didn't let go for the rest of the dream.*

*While showering, I saw two bruises on my left upper arm, the typical fingerprint-type bruises. —October 28, 2011 (end of Mayan calendar according to Carl Calleman)*

I believe Crote sent this message to me, as he knows I had been missing him. It was a reminder that there are those in the unseen world who know me, who love me, who are proud of me.

I have not seen Crote for about three years now. I do not understand why he left, why he has not returned, and it makes me quite sad. I can only hope I will see him again in the future.

\*\*\*

# Chapter 4
## Places: Tunnels and Caves

In 1987 my first husband and I spent a week in Hawaii, Oahu and Kauai, in a last-ditch attempt to revive our floundering marriage. One of my fondest memories of that week was the day we spent a day trip out of Kauai on a small catamaran, sailing to a tiny remote island with about six other passengers. There was a half-moon crescent of perfect white sandy beach where we spent the day snorkeling, swimming, and sunbathing. Later in the afternoon the beach was overshadowed when the sun went behind a sharp pointed mountain, remarkably similar to Bali Hai in *South Pacific*, and a guide showed us to a hidden cavern behind a ferny grotto. We stepped into the cavern and it led down stony steps to a wonderland, an enormous cavern lit with phosphorescent rocks. As my eyes adjusted to the light I could see the stalactites and stalagmites, and hear a distant dripping as they formed from the endlessly dripping mineral waters. There was a walkway alongside an underground lake, which led us to yet another sandy beach, this one in the darkness rather than sunshine, lit only by the phosphorescent rocks. We ventured into the fresh-water lake, which was warm, and playfully splashed and played in the water until we were told it was time to return on the catamaran before sunset. It was our best day in Hawaii.

He and I are not on particularly friendly terms but now that we share grandchildren we have let the water go under the bridge and are civil to each other at family gatherings. At one such gathering our daughter was planning a trip to Hawaii with her husband and two-year-old son. "We should tell them about that cool island where we spent the day, with the cave," I spoke to my ex-husband.

His reaction confused me. "What are you talking about, Donna? We didn't see any caves."

"You know," I continued. "When we took the catamaran for the day trip to that little island."

He looked entirely perplexed. "You are crazy. [Unfortunately, this was a phrase he employed often during our marriage.] We never took any day trips. And we didn't take any catamaran to any island. There are only the main islands in Hawaii, not little outer islands like you had in Florida."

My world went reeling. It was like being told I never lived in a certain house or held a certain job. I had distinct, cherished memories of that day on the island. I couldn't wait to get home and use the magic of Google Earth to prove him wrong. What I found was that I was the one who was wrong. There was no such island. There were no such day trips. There were similar type caverns in New Zealand, the Waitomo Glowworm Caves lit by bioluminescent worms, but definitely no such thing remotely near Hawaii.

I had to come face to face with some startling revelations. One, and this hit me the hardest, was that my memories are faulty. I began to question all my memories. How was I to know what was true? I placed a call to my second husband, my Florida husband. We are on much better terms in the way of friendship. We briefly exchanged small talk, then I got to the meat of the conversation. "You know how much I miss Weeki Wachee and our boating days there," I spoke wistfully. The Weeki Wachee River is my favorite place on Earth, and I count my happiest hours of my life there with my then-husband, our many dogs, and my daughter and her friends; swimming with manatees, playing with wild river otters, feeding raccoons on the riverbank, swimming in crystal-clear cool waters that stay 72 degrees year-round as they bubble fresh and pure from the depths of the Florida Aquifer, then course down the river on their way to the Gulf of Mexico. The water was refreshing in the steamy Florida summers of 95-degree weather with humidity in the 90s. There was a flash of adrenalin as alligators were known to swim there too, but were usually scared off by the boat motor. There was an abundance of glorious nature, everything from squirrels and wild birds to tiny minnows in the shallows that nibbled our toes and ate fried chicken from our fingers. Egrets, dragonflies, blue herons, frogs, salamanders, and countless others make their home at the Weeki Wachee Preserve, a natural habitat.

"Remember the tunnels there?" I ventured to ask.

"What tunnels?" he was munching on some food. My knees went weak and I had to sit down. NO. NOT WEEKI WACHEE TOO.

"You know," I tried to sound casual, "where the river takes a fork at those condos. We usually follow it to the left and go past the houses with the docks. But every once in a while we'd go to the right, past some cattails and other high vegetation, and find a kind of secret entrance to a tunnel. The river went right in there, and our boat just barely fit on the sides, but once inside it opened out into a big cavern that echoed. Usually there were a bunch of kids playing on the sand. It was real dark in there but lit up by some kind of glowing rocks in the ceiling of the cave."

There was an uncomfortably long silence on the other end.

"You still there?" I ventured to ask.

"Donna, I don't know what you're talking about. The river dead-ends at those cattails. Remember we tried one time to see what was on the other side of them, and we got stuck in the muck and had to get out and push the boat to get it turned around? There are no caves at Weeki Wachee. Don't know what to tell ya."

"Wow," I stumbled over my words, bereft of emotion. "Must have been some of my crazy dreams."

"Yeah, must have."

These memories were as real to me as the world I now look upon. They are not some flimsy floating vague recall of a dreamlike experience. They are real. Real, I tell you. More real than many of the "real" memories from my past that can be validated by other people. Everything about the caverns, the smell, the sound, the peals of children's laughter, the people with me … more real than the times I've visited Disneyland. And more fun.

There's another tunnel-and-cave place I've visited, at downtown State Street in Santa Barbara, where I grew up. I am no longer friends with the girl who was my best friend at that time, Gale, but we often took the public bus to shop downtown during summer vacation before we were old enough to drive. It stopped at a corner that allowed us easy access up and down the street where we could peer in to the shops and occasionally spend some cash. The tunnels are there too. Down on lower State Street past the old Granada Theater and just before it crosses Highway 101, toward the ocean and Stearns Wharf, there was a Pier 1 Imports store, one of my favorite stores of all. I loved the smell of baskets and incense and foreign markets. It has long since departed that location but I fondly recall a small stretch of shops just off the main street called Paseo Nuevo. It was decorated in old Spanish style, like the rest of the downtown area, with sidewalk cafes and quaint shops. At the very end of the Paseo Nuevo I recall a gated entrance that not everyone could find (though it was a six-foot-tall green gate). Gale and I used to open the gate and step inside, revealing tunnels filled with more shops. We had to step downward, going underground for a bit. The shops were more of an open-air environment in the darkened caves, lit by torches and glowing rocks, and vendors sold handmade candles, unique jewelry, clothing made of the softest cloth possible, and books written in an obscure language. I don't recall ever buying anything there, though once I was given some incense to take home and meditate with.

I am not able to call Gale and converse with her, but I have the powerful suspicion that the gate at the end of Paseo Nuevo does not now exist, nor did it ever. Not in this reality.

So what's the deal? How can I recall these times and places so vividly? Although the day in Hawaii was only a one-time event, I visited the shopping tunnels and the Weeki Wachee River tunnel frequently, probably at least a dozen times each.

I was given a description of reality once by the aliens, who tried to "dumb down" their version of reality to a level that I could understand. What I took from that was that reality is overlapping on many levels. Just as I sit here now and radio waves, TV waves, microwaves, and Wi-Fi waves are passing through my body, to which I am oblivious, there are other forms of reality that also coexist with us right here, right now, to which we are oblivious. They may or may not be aware of our existence. But I am convinced that those tunnels are there. They are in Santa Barbara, they are off the coast of Kauai, they are alongside the river in Weeki Wachee. It's just that we, in our limited human comprehension, are unable to see/hear/taste/smell/touch them. For some reason, maybe for the reason of eventually writing this book to tell others of it, I was occasionally allowed in.

The saddest thing of all is that once I accepted these places were not "real," I stopped visiting them. They contain some of the happiest memories of my life, and I went there with the people I loved. Now that those people are no longer in my life, I would at least go in my dreams and re-experience it, waking up to the happy thoughts that I was dreaming of old memories. Now the dreams have stopped. Such is the strength of our belief systems upon our waking—and sleeping—realities.

\*\*\*

## The Universal Library

Ever since I can remember I have taken classes in my dreams. Sometimes I am met by a teacher in a brown monk's robe who leads me to sit under an apple tree, the only tree in a vast field of rolling green hills. There is a meandering stream nearby, to which we walk and take a sip of water when thirsty or needing a break. The apples from the tree are the best I've ever tasted, red and sweet and crisp. But mostly we sit under the tree and he talks to me about things, important things, things that I try so hard to remember upon waking, but the memory of his teachings is whisked away from my mind like a cobweb brushed from a corner of the porch. Have I failed in not remembering the teachings? Are these things that my subconscious mind needs to know but not my conscious mind? It always feels so vastly important and I am aware, during the teachings, that it is very important that I remember these things. And yet I do not.

The other place where I am schooled is what I call the Universal Library. I have always loved libraries; the peace and quietude, the whispered voices, the smell of old books, the amount of knowledge contained with the walls and the thought of all the people who have come before me to learn. Is it because I have attended classes at the Universal Library for most of my life that I hold such reverence for libraries?

The Universal Library is a massive building, floating out in space. It simply rests in the blackness of space with stars all around. It's reminiscent of ancient Greek or Roman architecture with vast marble pillars out front, six in total. There are wide marble steps leading up to the enormous double wooden doors in front. I believe there are twelve steps. The doors swing out, surprisingly easy to pull despite their thickness and heavy weight. Once inside I can see there is no ceiling, no roof, but the library is well lit by a light source at the top, where the ceiling should be. This light source doesn't hurt my eyes and in fact invites me to look past it at the marvelous bright constellations above it. Inside the building are the hushed tones and scents of old books expected in a typical library, but at the forefront are tables, long tables, dozens of them, each with people intensely studying at them, reading out of large heavy ancient books. There are small children, old hunched men in pajamas, housewives in robes, teenagers in cheerleader uniforms. There are all races and ages, both genders. No one is paying any mind to anyone else; each person is intent on his or her own study. Many have what could be called an angel at their side, a person in a white robe sitting or standing, watching over them. I am always accompanied as well but I don't know who it is, as they always stand to my right and slightly behind me. I sense an incredible benevolence, kindness, love, and helpfulness. I never had a grandmother but I sense this is what a loving grandma would feel like, standing just behind me, her gentle hand softly at rest on my shoulder.

I am shown to a seat and books are brought to me. They are always large; sometimes just one, sometimes a stack of them, sometimes file folders. They are always Important with a capital I. They have to do with planning my life, with making major life decisions, or coping with the consequences of choices I have already made. In this Universal Library, I know, are all the answers. To everything. I have asked to walk the rows of books and have been allowed to do so, but when I reached for certain gold-embossed leather volumes a hand has gently pulled mine down, and I am given a message such as *Now is not the time* or *This is not for you to know*. I sense regret and even sorrow in their voice, as though they hold out hope that someday we humans will have the sense to be allowed to read these volumes. But we are not yet ready. Not me, not any of us. Not yet. I feel they hold the Secrets to the Universe. But I accept their judgment, knowing that they discipline us with love and justice.

\*\*\*

## Black Swimming Pools

There is a building with a massive indoor swimming pool that is all black. We humans stand on either side of the pool and are asked to jump in. The problem is, it is terrifying. The walls and floor of the

85

pool are black, the water itself appears black, and the surrounding atmosphere is dim. They will sometimes turn on the pool lights in an attempt to coerce us, and then a few humans do willingly jump in and swim to the other side, which is the objective for some reason, but the lights shining under the black water just makes the whole place creepier and more horrifying to me, as well as to many of the others who sometimes scream when the lights come on, or turn and hide their faces, or bury their hands in their faces. We are not prepared to swim; we are still dressed in whatever garb we happened to be in at the time of our abduction.

After a certain amount of time if we do not agree to go in the water, a few of us will be pushed in. I've been pushed in on multiple occasions. The water is the same temperature as the air and feels clean enough, like regular water, but it terrifies me to be in this dark place. When I was younger I was held down under the water until I breathed it in, literally drowning, until I realized I could somehow breathe in this fluid; it must be some type of liquid oxygen. Now I just swim to the other side as fast as I can and climb out, seemingly satisfying the aliens who have brought me here.

*** 

## Where Do They Come From?

Where do the aliens come from? They have given me various answers to that question—our future, their future, a distant planet, our inner Earth, an alternate dimension—and yet I don't believe they're purposefully deceptive. It is just so difficult to translate their reality into ours. If their sense of time is different from ours, and their physics are different from ours, then how can we relate on these and other levels?

They have shown me a lovely place that has a strong sense of "home" to me yet I am unsure if it's another planet or if it's right here, either inside Earth or right alongside us in a parallel dimension. My gut feeling says the parallel dimension theory is correct. It would also explain why they are so very concerned about our nuclear capabilities, as that would affect them powerfully. We have a very limited range of sight, sound, taste, touch, and smell. If reality is a pie, then we only sense a very small piece of the pie with our human senses. There could feasibly be entire other realities in that pie that we are unaware of, but they could possibly be aware of us on some level. When we sleep and dream, or go into a trance state or meditative state, we could expand our awareness to encompass some of that other reality. This is what I've been told.

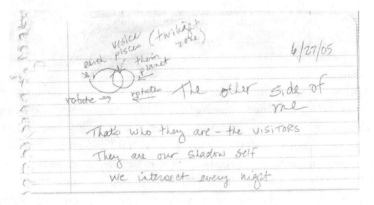

When I finally began to accept that these experiences were real, and that there was a good chance I was interacting with beings from an alternate reality or another planet or both, this is what they showed me one night in June 2005. Their planet is right next to ours, so close that they actually intersect with us. They rotate west to east, as opposed to our Earth rotating east to west. They are on a slightly smaller planet than ours, but of a different vibrational value so that it glides through ours without our even noticing it. They, however, are well aware of us especially because our wars and pollution and nuclear testing affects and disturbs them vibrationally. The vesica pisces, the place where our planets intersect, changes slightly every night because of their faster rate of rotation and due to the fact that their planet is smaller than ours. This is how they reach us more easily at certain times. They have begun calling it the *twilight zone* due to our human fascination with the irregularities it causes. This is usually the cause for what we think of as ghostly apparitions, déjà vu experiences, lost items, freak waves and storms, and other phenomena. If we could learn about them, accept what is happening, agree to stop disrupting all of nature, which includes them and their world, then things would greatly change in our world for the better.

In addition to the twilight zone vesica pisces world above, I am frequently taken to a place that looks like a planet as we approach it; a very small planet in which I can see the curve of the horizon as we come in closely, and it appears to be covered in beautiful turquoise seas. There are what I call mashed-potato islands, land that looks like clumps of mashed potatoes piled up high on top of the water. As we pull in closer to one of the mashed-potato lumps, I see that it forms a horseshoe-shaped area where the ground is level, and it is covered with glistening pinkish-white sand. This is where we land. I have swum in the warm, clear seas there, having been told there are no sharks or other predatory or harmful animals present. The water is very buoyant, more so than our oceans, so that I simply float without any effort whatsoever. Once back on the beach, I see that there is a cave-like entrance into the mashed potatoes. I walk over to touch them and of course they are not soft and potato-like but rather are solid like rock. I (along with my ever-present companions to the side and slightly to the rear of me so I can't see them) enter the cave, bringing me to a fairyland of rocks that glow softly, lighting the way along a twisty path that heads downward. It is quite a distance down before I come upon an underground river that also glows, further lighting the cave. Between the glowing rocks and the glowing water it has a comfortable well-lit atmosphere. It is cool but not uncomfortably so. The air is fresh and slightly breezy. Soon I hear the lilting laughter of small children, and the path takes a turn, opening onto a gigantic room with high ceilings from which several waterfalls pour, forming a large lake in the center of the room. All around the outside of the lake people are sitting, conversing, enjoying their time together. Children, and some adults, are playing in the water, sliding down the rock slides and waterfalls. It is truly a magical, joyful place. People recognize me and come excitedly over to see me, greeting me with hugs, taking me by the hand so I will join them. I often play with the children in the lake and I particularly love the rock slide. There are other tunnels leading away from the lake, lit by the surrounding rocks, which I understand lead to living quarters and other areas. Sometimes I venture down one of them that comes to an open-air (or open-cave as it were) market, kind of like a farmer's market, where odd-looking fruits and vegetables are sold, as well as beautiful jewelry made from unusual shells and crystals, books, and other goods, each with a proud and friendly vendor. I sometimes buy some of the jewelry for my people back here on Earth, but when I awaken it is never with me. I do have one trinket, a small silver dolphin attached to a clear quartz crystal, which simply appeared in my jewelry box about 1992 and I have no recall of having bought it. Could it be I was actually able to bring it "home" here?

I found a drawing I had done entitled HOME, shown below. Unfortunately, it's undated but I believe it was done around 2005, at the time I was beginning to accept the reality of their presence and their places. I was considering the fact that I may have originally come from another planet, or belonged on another planet somehow, in some way. This mashed-potato island place felt like "home" to me like no place on Earth had ever felt. In the drawing I show two suns and three moons. *One big reddish moon (looks like Jupiter); one small moon, white like Earth's moon; and one medium-sized moon, greenish and hazy.*

On the same paper I had drawn yet another alien creature, this one an inhabitant of the mashed-potato island home. The inhabitants are *covered with "velvet" softness, have beautiful cat-like faces, only four fingers because five is the number of man and they are not human, dog ears that are velvety soft, a tail which wags to express emotion and ends in a tuft of hair. They have suction-like fingers like a tree frog and pointy feet which they use to "swim" in the air, they don't walk. They make sounds like our dolphins or whales.* I am uncertain of their size. I don't believe they come to Earth but rather stay on their beautiful home and occasionally host humans and other beings there.

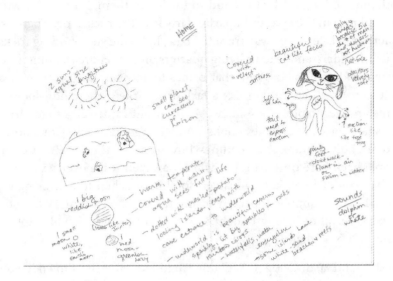

When it is time to leave, my Grey companions come to get me and I never want to go. This is where the bruising on my upper arms often occurs. I don't want to leave. This place is utter paradise—simple, free, happy, joyful, comfortable. Why would I want to leave? They try sending me images of my family back home, my grandchildren, my dog, but even with that I want to stay. So they draw me away, and the family and friends I have there seem to understand and pull back, saying goodbye, waving bravely. I know I have family there, possibly even children of my own, but they accept that I must come back here. I usually cry the whole way home, and when I wake in my bed I am generally sad or nostalgic or melancholy for several hours. A big part of this is that I am not allowed to recall their faces. Their bodies are slightly blurred, but their faces are entirely blank or absent in my mind by the time I wake, except for the one time I saw the being above. I don't know if that is what my "family" looks like or not. All I know is they are beautiful, far more beautiful than our creepy primate human faces. Humans are so prideful, we think we are the best thing in the universe, but I know better. I know we are considered barbaric, primitive, vengeful, unforgiving, harsh, and really quite ugly by the majority of the aliens. Once, *January 24, 2012*, I was so distraught upon leaving that one of the Greys turned to me and told me telepathically, **Your home planet is called Halix** (pronounced Hay-licks). I am assuming that lovely small mashed-potato-island planet with three moons and two suns is Halix. He refused to give me any further information and I'm guessing he broke the rules by telling me the name; even Greys can have compassion at times. I googled Halix the next morning only to find it's a creature in a video game; also there's a monster truck with that name. There are no planets called Halix—in our known star systems.

✳✳✳

## Bathrooms

For some obscure reason the aliens are fascinated by toilets and by our toileting functions. Often the scenes are of public toilets, crowded stalls, and usually they are utterly filthy. I suppose they're trying to instill strong emotions in us with these scenes. Unfortunately, my dreams often involve all five senses, and the aliens are sure to include the appropriate smells to add to the realism. A couple of times I have actually vomited in these horrific public bathrooms.

*The digestive tract is a whole new concept for them and they are fascinated by it. Many many of my experiences have involved toilets and public restrooms, and for some reason they are usually filthy. Are they trying to get an extreme emotional response from me?*

*Many people who struggle with lifelong bladder infections and/ or irritable bowel do so because this is their first organic life with a digestive system or urinary system. Trees don't need to pee! —March 2014*

Because the aliens do not have gastrointestinal systems, they are intrigued by ours. They do not urinate or defecate so they want to know everything about us and why we have elimination from our bodies. They do not have genitals and are therefore fascinated with ours and our sexuality.

Very often these dreams of public bathrooms are in my old high school—perhaps because high school holds vivid memories in my mind. In reality my high school was newly built and the bathrooms were spotless, but in these dreams they are filthy and disgusting: feces smeared on the walls, bloody tampons piled in the corner or strewn around the floor, toilets clogged with urine, paper, feces. I leave the stall to go to another and it is the same, if not worse, with flies buzzing around the piles of shit on the floor. In about half of these dreams my sense of smell kicks in and it is extremely realistic, causing me to gag and retch. Sometimes I feel such a desperation to urinate that I attempt to squat over the horrific toilet to pee, and while my pants are down around my ankles a cheerleader or other popular girl will reach over the door and steal my purse from the hanger. I believe the aliens are trying to instill various emotions in me (and it works)—emotions like repulsion, anger, frustration, and a vague sense of fear, of wanting to get the hell out of there and find my way home. I believe they are studying a vast range of our emotions, they are trying to understand all of them, and I can't believe I volunteered for these experiences but somewhere deep down inside I know I did.

Bathrooms of all types seem to be fair game for their tests. Campsite outhouses, giant public bathrooms, the bathroom at my home, all come into play at various times. On rare occasions they are spotlessly clean, but most often they are covered in some kind of grime or filth. I seriously have no answers as to why I am forced to experience this.

\*\*\*

## Portals

I have wondered why the aliens frequently come in through a door, through a window, out of a closet. If they have the ability to float through walls, why the theatrics of making an entrance through a doorway? I came to this conclusion: They interact with our world partially through our minds; it's one of the ways they adjust their frequency to that of our reality. In our minds, doors, windows, and closets are portals. The window is a portal from inside to outside. The closet is a portal from a small storage space to the outer room. It then becomes easier for the aliens to present themselves through a portal, and it provides a dual purpose as aiding our human minds to accept what is happening to us—it is acceptable in our reality for someone to come in through a door so when our mind sees an alien coming through a doorway it is not quite as *alien* to us as seeing it float through the wall; our mind is slightly more willing to accept what it is seeing.

In the home my second husband and I shared they frequently appeared in the bedroom closet. I saw small Greys peering out from the closet depths like eager little children on Christmas morning, excited to see if I was asleep or, if awake, if I would readily accept their presence (I was starting to). This same house had what looked like a large black laundry chute through which they deposited me when they were finished with me. More than once I woke up with an "uff" as the air was knocked out of me after sliding down this "laundry chute" that opened up through a flap in the bedroom ceiling above my side of the bed. I fell from the ceiling to the bed and sometimes landed so roughly that my back was painful the next day. Sometimes it woke my husband up, but he would drowsily return to sleep, oblivious of my journey, probably anesthetized by the aliens.

*I was at the cave at Weeki Wachee and being shown an old parchment map, entrances and exits pointed to by an old long wizened finger, marked by spirals, some clockwise and some counterclockwise. I was told the limestone under Florida made more holes; therefore easier to travel the portals.*

*The trees also have something to do with the portals. —October 30, 2012, full moon, day of Hurricane Sandy*

***

## Ships

*Many dreams of being in a round movie theater with heavy red velvet draperies, or a huge round building with red velvet carpeting. Stairs spiral down and then back up to the top with no way out. It's like being inside a snail shell whose bottom leads back to the top. — January 12, 2003*

I have been on countless ships. There is no standard appearance; each one is completely different and seemingly has a life and occupants of its own. Many are round and I have found that my screen memories are of round buildings, round cars, round trains, round elevators, glass elevators. One common theme is red; round rooms covered in heavy red velvet draperies like an old-fashioned movie theater—only round.

*I worked in a big round bank. Our boss was mean. I had to work until after dark and then carry two heavy grocery bags two miles to my car in the dark. I started to leave but had to go back because I forgot my purse. Our boss was sitting at a round table talking to someone. When he saw me listening he beckoned me over and smiled. He was Asian and had Chinese or Japanese-looking tattoos on both ankles. He was barefoot and his feet were deformed like they had been tightly bound when he was a baby. —December 10, 2002*

Again in 2002 I had a vivid dream of being given a tour of the inside of a craft. Two entities walked at my sides and just behind me. I often feel a slight hand pressure on my shoulder or upper arm as they guide me along, as I seem to be floating or gliding but not walking, as though I am a balloon; weightless. In this particular experience I was taken from a small hallway into a giant room, about the size of a large warehouse, and it was stacked with rows upon rows of glass "jars" that were each about five feet tall, stacked three high. I looked down a long row and didn't see the end of the jars. Each jar contained a giant pear marinating in fluid. There were tubes attached to the jars, and the entire chamber echoed with a type of breathing sound as the fluid swished in and out of the tubes, apparently keeping the giant pears fresh. The entities with me were very proud; they didn't say much but

I understood that this was a special area that most humans are not shown. They now trusted me, and I was learning to trust them, so this was confirmation of our blossoming relationship.

When I awoke it was very clear to me that those were not pears. They were fetuses. They looked human, curled up in fetal positions with the cords swooshing fluids and nutrients and oxygen to them in lieu of an actual umbilical cord, but it's possible they were not human, or possibly not fully human.

This is a classic example of a "screen memory" that the aliens implant in our minds. Jars of pears, giant pears; it made perfect sense to me at the time they were shown to me. Yet when awake and reviewing the experience, it made no sense at all. I believe it was the swooshing sounds, which very much sounded like the heartbeat heard through a Doppler fetal monitor, which clued me in. The veil began to drop as I came to accept that these experiences were real.

I had a hysterectomy in 1993 but my ovaries were left intact. It is possible that they continued to harvest eggs from me until October 2001 when I needed to have my ovaries removed. Is it possible that one—or several—of these fetuses belonged to me? Is that why they showed them to me with such pride and a sense of secrecy that I was somehow special in being allowed to see this place?

I am not a technical person or an engineer so I am unable to understand their ships' technology to explain in more detail. The aliens interact with us telepathically, utilizing our own brains to communicate. I am a highly emotional person so my primary means of communication with the aliens is emotional. I apologize for being unable to provide more of a technical explanation for what I have seen inside the ships.

The ships have various rooms: the large white round rooms act as a holding area for the abductees; the examination rooms are stark white with only a stainless-steel-looking table in the center, and instruments appear out of the nothingness of the walls and ceiling; the giant warehouse rooms house vats of fetuses with their humming, pulsating nourishment tubes. One room is a flight center, where if I am very lucky I am allowed to observe and sometimes even briefly take the controls of the ship. This is not a particularly large room but has about twelve alien beings in it; two Greys at the center controls and other beings performing odd jobs around the room, on the ceiling, scurrying about the floor. The viewing window can either be totally transparent, or can be opaque all except a small window. Usually it is large and wide open, as the aliens are curious and intelligent beings who like to see what is going on around them. Once I was fortunate enough to sit at the controls next to a surprisingly friendly female Grey in her controller's seat, and she seemed to enjoy my fright as we cruised at thousand-miles-an-hour speeds right through houses, trees, cars, buildings, even a mountain. She explained telepathically that at that speed our vibrational rate was different from those of solid objects and thus we simply passed right through them. To demonstrate she slowed us down and we headed directly toward the corner of a house. I was horrified that we were going to have a terrible crash, but we simply hit it with a gentle bump as we floated softly in the air. She laughed—or what I consider to be laughing by a Grey alien. I then laughed also— once the barrier of fear comes down we can have fun together, get to know one another, experience reality through one another's eyes.

***

# Chapter 5
## Evidence

*I think I have found a kind of "proof" of visitation. We have glow-in-the-dark stars on our bedroom ceiling. They absorb light when it's available, either from the sun shining through the window or from artificial light; then they glow after the light source is gone. When we first turn off the lights to go to sleep they glow very brightly for 15 to 20 minutes, gradually diminishing. So if I wake up at 1 a.m., the room is pitch black (my husband likes to keep it real dark). The darkness used to terrify me, but now I can get up and go to the restroom in the blackness—a real milestone for me.*

*A month or so ago I woke up at 3 a.m. hearing a ship pulling up and away. I was hyperventilating. It sounded like the revving of jet engines in reverse, then quickly moving away. "What's that? What's that?" I remember trying to scream as I caught my breath, so the words came out very quietly. My husband mumbled something in his sleep so I said, "Don't you hear that?" as the engine sound took off upwards and outwards.*

*Annoyed, he replied, "I don't hear anything. Go back to sleep!"*

*But I knew the visitors had just been here, and just as I had become conscious a beam of intense blue light had been beamed at me from a corner of the bedroom; the same corner I frequently find myself standing in when I wake from sleepwalking. I lay there feeling that familiar combination of terror, curiosity, aloneness, and more terror, added to the fear that I was losing my grip on reality. I lay flat on my back, wide awake, eyes open. Just then it occurred to me that the ceiling stars were glowing brightly. I turned to the clock on my nightstand. 3:33. Those lights should not be glowing; we had gone to bed hours ago. This meant the blue light had been REAL because the stars picked up its luminescence!*

*As per usual, these moments had faded to obscurity in my mind by morning. But last night's events are real to me. I was deeply asleep when an unknown male voice had told me, in an irresistible monotone, "turn over ... turn over ... turn over ... turn over," each time becoming louder and more insistent. Finally through a haze of unconsciousness I heard myself saying, "No! I don't want to roll over!" I was sound asleep and comfortable!*

*This awakened my husband, who asked, "Why are you yelling at me?"*

*I replied, "Why do you want me to roll over?" Though I was aware on some level that it hadn't been his voice, I was in that state of mental confusion that is induced by something alien touching my mind.*

*"You're crazy, I never said anything!" he answered, promptly returning to deep sleep, snoring lightly.*

*Suddenly my gut clenched in fear and a buzzing in my right ear confirmed that not only had they recently been there, they were still there. It was 12:39 p.m. and I knew they weren't finished with me yet. Fighting the terror, I willed conscious contact but had to close my eyes because it was too much to look, too overwhelming to guess what I might see. Behind my closed eyelids, their faces danced. The next thing I knew I was slowly becoming conscious, struggling to scream, aware of the blue light in the corner. The clock read 3:33 a.m. And the ceiling stars were brightly glowing. —October 22 (no year)*

*Woke up and the entire right half of the bedroom was bathed in a deep purple, 3-D, with glowing points of light like distant stars. I turned away to look at the window to get my bearings and when I turned back the purple was gone. It had been luminous, glowing, yet deep—a color I had never seen before. —August 23, 2002*

\*\*\*

## Foretelling the Future

There have been many dreams in which it seemed I was writing nonsense, yet in retrospect, sometimes after years of retrospect, I see they were predicting my future. Since time is different for them, perhaps they were just stating facts that were true for them at their present time. Here is an example:

*I was with my husband at an observatory in the mountains. There were other people there; it was a class or something about the stars. They found out an asteroid was coming directly at us that night. We got some supplies at an Army store and got ready in the mountains. But I got to thinking about the dogs all alone, and they would be scared and starve to death. Rather than saving myself in the mountains I wanted to take my chances at home. I tried to wake my husband up but he would not listen or wake up so I went by myself. I stole someone's Jeep and took off for home, hoping it was not too late. —April 9, 2003*

It seems they use threats like impending meteors and nuclear attacks to get my attention and help me remember dreams that otherwise would have gone unnoticed. In this case, my marriage was seemingly fine on this date; however, we ended up being divorced by February 2005 and I felt like "I was unable to wake him up and he would not listen." A couple of years later I took our last surviving dog and "headed home" to California. About a year after that my daughter gave me her old Jeep when I ran into financial difficulties. So now I am "home" with a "Jeep" and "taking care of my dog." Apparently it's not too late!

## Bruises

*I had a wake-up-screaming episode (which I had three con-secutive last week, and my daughter has been having mysterious bruising including upper arms like mine). I "dreamed" various vague things but especially that someone was taking off and put-ting on shoes and socks* [on me]. *I was about 2 or 3 years old and it felt like my mother's gentle touch, but she had trouble with my left foot and I kept clenching my toes.*

*Later that morning when I went to take a shower I saw a dark gray spot about ¼ inch oval covering the tip of my left big toe. It won't wash off. —March 25, 2001*

*The mark at the tip of my left toe has faded to a crescent moon shape. —March 26, 2001*

Over the years I've awakened with numerous bruises and other strange markings. To the best of my knowledge I don't recall a "tracking device" being installed as other abductees have, though I've had many instruments shoved up my nose and have awakened with nosebleeds more times than I can count. Whenever things got to be too much for me, Crote, who was standing by my side, would extend his left hand and place it on my forehead. I would either instantaneously be unconscious or would go out of body and not feel anything the body was experiencing as I watched from a safe distance, floating above. Here is a picture of my inner right thigh taken March 12, 2011, clearly showing bruising from three fingers and a thumb from an extended frog-like hand.

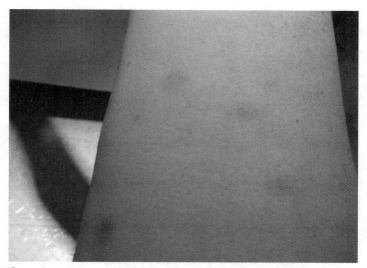

These bruises were a frequent part of the abductions but I rarely took photos; primarily because I wasn't ready to accept what was really happening. In 2005 I had just divorced, and was living in a house with my twenty-something daughter and we often both woke up with the mysterious frog-hand bruising on our upper arms. It was about this point I was beginning to accept the reality of what was happening to me, and now also to her, but when I broached the subject with her she got uncomfortable and changed the conversation to something benign and easier to accept. I never pushed her. It was easier for me to accept that I was undergoing this experience than to know that she was too. You want to protect your children, and somehow I felt like it was my fault if they took her too—why didn't I protect her (not that I could stop it anyway)? Did they take her because she is my daughter? Is it something in our DNA that they want? Are they going to take my grandchildren too?

The upper arm bruising is on the fleshy part of the upper inner arm, usually two or three fingerprints and sometimes a thumb. The hand and fingers appear to be about the size of a six-year-old's hand. In my vague, hazy recall I am usually accompanied by two Greys, one on each side of me, guiding me out of bed, down hallways and into rooms, up onto exam tables. I can see how it causes bruising.

101

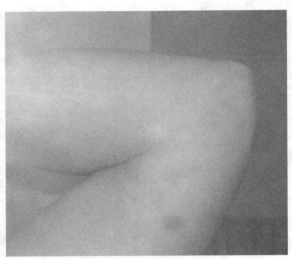

This is a poor picture, taken in a mirror on April 12, 2010, but shows the two distinct fingerprints near my elbow. One is a different color than the other, causing me to wonder if one of the fingers, probably the middle longer one, is stronger than the others.

There have also been injection sites and triangle-shaped markings. Here's a triangle-shaped site, possibly an injection, on the inner part of my right ankle taken on September 15, 2011. These markings are always painless but sometimes a little itchy. Even the bruises are painless, though they look like they would hurt.

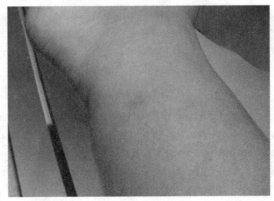

Evidence

For years I believed that when I was taken, it was my spirit or soul or consciousness or essence that they took, leaving my heavy earthly body paralyzed in the bed. Wouldn't my husband or family notice if I was gone for a couple of hours, even if it was the middle of the night while everyone was asleep? I have no satisfactory answers, but have a few theories:

> They really do take my physical body. They paralyze or anesthetize the rest of the household and take me.

> They take everyone in the bedroom and/or everyone in the household.

> They take only my consciousness, leaving my body paralyzed and slumbering in the bed, but my body is physically aware of the incidents and feels them. In the same way a hypnotist can convince persons they are holding a hot coal in their hand and actually raise up blisters, though there is nothing in the hand, my body remembers what my consciousness experienced, and this results in bruises and markings.

These are only my feeble theories. I have no idea what the truth is. The truth is apparently too alien for my limited human mind to accept.

\*\*\*

## Laying the Groundwork

*I was told that me and my soul group came to **lay the groundwork**—to till the soil, level it, remove weeds—**and then my daughter and her soul group would "plant the seeds"**—literally their seeds; their children. It is a new stage in evolution. —February 19, 2003*

I found this slightly humorous as my daughter, age twenty-four at the time this was written, was firmly ensconced in the idea that she would never marry and would definitely never have children. Her

103

lifestyle was such that I believed her. Incredibly, she fell crazy in love, had a baby, and got married in 2009. She had a second baby three years later. Yet another prediction by the aliens which I had little faith in has come to pass; she is now "planting the seeds" of the next phase in evolution. All of her friends are having babies too; indeed there seems to have been quite a baby boom from about 2009 to the present. Additionally, my niece (who I believe is in my daughter's soul group) had sworn that she would never have children. She miraculously had a medically difficult but successful pregnancy in 2006. Each of these children seem to be wise old souls, interested in healing at a young age, highly intuitive and intelligent. With all the talk of Indigo and Crystal children becoming incarnate on Earth, it gives me great hope for a positive future of our dear planet.

\*\*\*

# Chapter 6
## Interactions | Awakening

*Before you awaken, you are asleep. Awakening comes in endless forms; not all recognizable. Sometimes we think we are awake but we are still dreaming. Sooner or later, each of us must awaken. We cannot sleep forever.*

*Awakening means clearing the cobwebs out of your eyes. It means opening your eyes and really seeing what is all around you. Are you afraid of the dark? Or are you afraid of the light?*

*When you are a child you can call for Mommy or Daddy and not feel so all alone, scared, and small. But once you're all grown up you are expected to get up, get dressed, do the morning commute and go to work as if nothing is ever wrong. Don't bring your personal problems to work, they say. But you are a person, how can you separate personal problems into segmented compartments like that? As a society we wonder how murderers and rapists can commit such cold-blooded crimes, apparently feeling no empathy or compassion for their victims, yet isn't that exactly what society is telling us to do, telling us to separate our emotional bodies from our physical bodies, from our mental and spiritual bodies? We are told to do exactly that; yet when people do it successfully they are called sociopaths. You are supposed to just take a pill when your stomach hurts instead of taking the time to listen to your body and perhaps realize your stomach hurts because you yelled at your preschooler while you were eating breakfast and you didn't have the time to apologize to her, telling her that you were anxious about being late for work and weren't really mad at her at all? So you sent her off to daycare in tears, and you popped a pill to make the stomachache go away. But the angst of yelling at your beloved child and making her cry, then leaving the issue unresolved, has not gone away. It is just burrowed into the folds of your stomach, and buried deeper into your subconscious mind. And into hers, the mind and heart of that precious toddler.*

*I am awakening and not without a fight. Sometimes we are awakened by a gentle tap on the shoulder. Sometimes a slap on the back. Sometimes an earthquake jolts us out of bed and throws us on the hard cold floor. Sometimes a car accident forces us to take a step back from life and look at things differently. As for me, I'm picking myself up off the floor, rubbing the sleep out of my eyes, and cleaning up the broken stuff after the earthquake. And you? Are you waiting for the next disaster to befall you, or will you pay attention to the gentle whisper in your ear saying, "Wake up! It's a new day!" —undated, circa 1980s when my child was a toddler and I was beginning to awaken to a new reality*

\*\*\*

One of the most disturbing aspects of my alien interactions is the concern that I am not the only one they seek. If they do follow certain family lineages as I've read, does that mean they want my daughter? My grandchildren? I don't want my loved ones to suffer from anything, ever. I especially don't want them to suffer the terrifying experiences I have endured … and yet there is a part of me that is grateful for the experiences, for the spiritual gifts I have been given, for the otherworldly friends and expansive outlook on life that they have brought to me. If the aliens have learned how to make contact without the horrifying aspects, then I would be okay with it … I think.

*I had a dream that my 4-year-old grandson and I were on a spaceship that looked like a hospital inside. The aliens took him, put him in a hospital bed, and started taking blood from him. I was very upset, yelling at them, but my grandson didn't mind at all and told me it was okay. Then one of the aliens explained to me that he was VERY SPECIAL and they needed his blood so that they could clone his heart; then they are going to put his cloned heart into thousands of other people so that they will have a beautiful, special, loving, generous heart like he does. —April 5, 2014, the night before his 5th birthday*

The fact that he wasn't terrified and in fact was calming me down was reassuring. He is a special child, wise beyond his years, but I still feel protective and don't like the idea of aliens messing about with him.

*** 

By meeting with us one-on-one they come to understand our struggles, our emotions, our compassion and empathy. They understand that we are vastly complicated beings physically, mentally, emotionally, and spiritually. They have learned that, while looking upon humanity en masse we may seem careless, destructive, violent, and hopeless; as individuals we are smart, caring, loving, and capable. We are a species worth saving after all.

You may have been reading my story and thinking, "That's all fine and good for Donna, but what if I want to see them? Talk to them?" I'm here to tell you that you can; that's one of the primary reasons I wrote this book. Conscious interaction can be attained with the aliens. They want to connect with us; they want to develop conscious relationships with us. Apparently time is of the essence so they want me to get this message out to as many people as I can.

Aliens interact with people all the time. By "people" I mean that term in the broadest sense, as the Native Americans used it, to include we two-legged people as well as four-legged, six-legged, eight-legged, winged, and rooted people. In other words, all lifeforms. I don't want to freak you out with the thought that aliens are spying on you constantly. They drop in for visits and then they leave. After all, we are not their sole reason for living. They have a world and a life outside of Earth. But they are fascinated with us and want to know us better. They do want to interact with the appropriate two-leggeds but often cannot due to fear. We live with so much fear in our hearts; so much anxiety, worry, and fear in our daily lives that this needs to be reduced as much as possible for health reasons as well as clear communication with aliens. Meditation, spending time in nature, gratitude for what you have, all help to alleviate the fear. Turn off the evening news and play with a puppy instead. If you have a hard time being grateful for anything, be grateful you are breathing. Be grateful you can read this page. Start small. Worry and fear can be habitual thoughts learned from parents, spouses, friends, and society in general. Be aware of your thoughts and whenever a fearful thought pops up, counteract it with a thought of love or gratitude or forgiveness. Fear comes disguised as anger, frustration, guilt, shame, jealousy. If it doesn't feel good, switch that emotion out for one that does. At first it takes conscious awareness but slowly as love replaces fear in your heart, it becomes more of a positive habit. When you have more love in your heart it is easier for the aliens to connect with you because they come from a place of love and peace and tranquility.

Additionally, there is a free-will arrangement; if you did not agree to interact with them prior to your birth like I did, you must give your conscious permission to interact with them now. You must ask them to visit, as they will not violate your free will. Many abductees claim they never gave permission and all they want is for the visitation to stop; I can't speak for them but I also felt that way myself for many years. Why the hell would I agree to something so terrifying, so *alien*? But as I've explained, over the years the aliens lessened my fear and increased my understanding to the point that I now realize I was obliging all along; otherwise, it never would have happened. They have given me an expanded worldview, a deep sense of spirituality, a depth of gratitude for our Earth, a love of nature, and an appreciation for all of life that I would not have otherwise had. I feel that, without the alien interventions that woke me up, I would have been sleepwalking through my life.

Aliens can read your heartfelt intentions. You need to demonstrate positive intent; you can't be planning to manipulate others or to cause others fear or harm with your alien connections. By others I not only mean other people; I mean your local environment and the larger environment as well. Make your intention for the highest and best good of all involved. They are looking for those who are pure of heart. I'm not implying that I am any better or holier-than-thou because they visit me. I tell the occasional white lie. I get angry in traffic. I'm no saint. I have done plenty of things I am not proud of. I eat meat at times, I pump deadly gasoline into my car. I even wished a boy would die when I was a kid and he actually got run over by a car and died a few months later. I'm not saying that I caused it, but it sure scared me into never wishing that again for anyone.

Looking back over my history, I see that during certain dark times in my personal life the aliens did not visit me. They stayed away because my thoughts were not of the best intent. I had the most contact in my life in 2005, the year I was facing divorce but didn't want it, and was focusing on emotional healing, forgiveness, and love for my then-husband. I was focused on love mostly. And they visited a lot.

They want to have relationships with us, with me and with you if that is what you desire. But there are a few rules:

1. Try not to be afraid. This is easier said than done when you wake up to a seven-foot-tall praying mantis standing at the foot of your bed.

2. Ask. Ask to see them, ask to hear them, ask for proof of their presence. Keep asking. Then be alert for even the smallest of signs. There is no such thing as coincidence you know.

3. Show your good intent by doing good works. Help an old lady cross the street. Pick up trash at a local park. Rescue a lost pet. Hug a tree. Tell some wildflowers that you appreciate their beauty (and mean it). Visit a children's hospital. Recycle. Rescue a spider, putting it outside on a plant instead of flushing it down the toilet. I'm not saying to do all of these things, but do what feels right in your heart. Lead with your feelings. Each of us has our individual gifts to give.
Then don't Tweet or Facebook about how generous you are or how wonderful you've been for rescuing your neighbor's pet; this is to be heartfelt activity between you and your Creator, not an excuse to stroke your ego. Do it just for the sake of doing it, showing your positive heartfelt intent to make the world a better place in both large and small ways.

4. If you feel drawn to crystals, you can raise your vibration by surrounding yourself with them. If you are fortunate enough to have a rock shop or metaphysical shop nearby, go and hold different crystals in your hand, touch them, close your eyes to feel the energy. They don't have to be big expensive ones. I prefer smaller ones that I can hold in my hand when I go to sleep, or the sharper ones that go under my pillow. By some accounts, having a piece of meteorite in your home will attract ETs. I have a small piece from the Meteor Crater near Winslow, Arizona, that I keep in my bedroom.

There are also things beyond our control that are said to attract alien intervention. These are hearsay only and cannot be confirmed:

1. Those with Rh negative blood are supposed to be more likely to be abducted. I personally have Rh positive blood,   not negative.

2. Being of Native American ancestry or Celtic ancestry. Most indigenous people have creation stories that include Star People. My Celtic heritage includes a Scottish grandmother, a great-grandmother from Wales, another great-grandmother from Ireland, and the rest are from England except for one great-grandfather who is a bit of a mystery.

3. Having a parent in the military. I was born near an Air Force base and lived on bases until age seven. My dad was a pilot and flight instructor for the Royal Canadian Air Force. He was stationed at Greenwood, Nova Scotia, when my night terrors, sleepwalking, and earliest memories of aliens began. This was in the early 1960s. We left Nova Scotia in the summer of 1965, and it was 1967 when the Shag Harbour incident occurred with reports of USOs, underwater submersible objects, around Nova Scotia.1 I have repeatedly asked my dad if he ever saw any craft, airborne or submersible, and he denies it. I wonder if he has suppressed memories, screen   memories, or was somehow hypnotized or drugged to forget anything that he might have seen.

The aliens have given me two good reasons why they won't come knocking at my front door (because believe me, I have asked them to do just that on multiple occasions. How it would simplify everything if I could just call my local TV station and ask them to send a camera crew to my house!). This is what they have told me:

1. *We humans are a lower vibration than they are, because we still reside with the seven deadly sins, i.e. lust, greed, gluttony, sloth, vanity, envy, pride. This keeps us down. If you had a pond of fly-infested slimy pig shit on one side of you, and a crystal clear pool on the other, which one would you immerse yourself in? For some unknown reason humanity continues to choose the slime of*

111

*nuclear waste, plastics in the ocean, and other "pig shit." Despite this, the aliens can recognize each one of us individually because of our unique vibration/ color. Our thoughts, conscious and unconscious, swirl around our heads like bees swarming a hive. Our brain is the hive, our thoughts the bees. When we sleep, the ego gets out of the way, the thoughts lessen, and the aliens can lower their vibration enough to reach us. However, they don't want to stay down too long, soaking in that fearful pit in which we immerse ourselves daily.*

2. *We are* **"brutal violent primitive animals surviving on base instincts."** *We could easily harm or kill their frail physical forms.*

*Earth was meant to be a true Garden of Eden physically, mentally, emotionally, and spiritually. It has the capability to be that way again.*
—*October 2014*

They have explained to me that humans have built a kind of wall around the Earth with their fear; a barrier that is nearly impenetrable by other beings who do not exist at the level of fear. There are pinpoints of light shining through this dark wall of fear however; and those pinpoints belong to those who have escaped the dark mindset of continual fear, or have the intention to do so. Looking at Earth from space, it appears to be a dark foggy barrier surrounding the planet with pinpoints of light sparkling through. Each pinpoint is a being striving to live in the light; striving to live more in awareness, love, and compassion than in fear. This includes animal and plant life; it is not strictly reserved for humans. But the humans who attempt to live in this way shine the brightest because we have the most to overcome. Watching from space, the aliens have shown me that some lights flicker as the person waxes and wanes between discouragement and faith; some shine off and on like blinking Christmas lights; and a very very few keep a constant brightness. Often these are people of strong faith, whether it be in religion, angels, faith in their fellow man, faith in themselves, faith in a higher power. That belief shines through strongly. When the light is stronger than the darkness, then the aliens will be more easily able to connect with us on a physical level. They have much wisdom to impart to us, and technology for healing our physical bodies and the planet we live on, which they are eager to share, but not until we are ready.

I would love for you to use my experiences, my trials and errors, as a jumping-off point for your own interactions with aliens so that you don't have to start at the beginning like I did. Rather than being naïve and uncertain, as I was, you can use this information to explore further and deeper into the inner and outer reaches of our reality.

\*\*\*

## What Is Reality?

Reality is subjective. What I call "red" may be a color you call "orange" and we would both be right, in our own realities. What the aliens have taught me is that there is a different reality for everyone alive. That tree in your front yard has a different reality than you do. You have a different reality than your spouse or your child, though their realities are more in common with yours than that of the tree. The most important thing the aliens have taught me is that no one is wrong, even those dwelling in darkness. It's supposed to be that way. Each of us is experiencing our own reality and learning at our own pace. Each one of us is a spark of our Creator experiencing the world. The Creator is experiencing the world through you as you. The Creator is experiencing the world through me as Donna. The Creator is experiencing the world as a tree through your tree.

Since this is a very complicated subject and I am no scientist or physicist or theologian, they tried to dumb it down for me, and the following illustration is the best they gave me after a long night of study with them on the concepts of reality. They describe Reality with the capital R as a circle—no beginning, no end. Infinite, always present. They then showed me inside my reality as another circle, smaller but not a lot smaller than the Big Reality. They colored me as green for simplicity's sake since they identify us by our aura colors. I prefer to see myself as turquoise blue like the Caribbean Sea but for this lesson they chose to make me green.

Now though I am a complete circle unto myself, not needing anyone or anything else to complete me. In order to experience the Big Reality I need to create some openings in my reality. I then use these openings to experience the world via my five senses of sight, hearing, taste, touch, and smell. They demonstrated each of these as a separate pie-wedge in my circle of reality, each vibrating at a different wavelength and different color. As a human, these are the tools I use to experience Reality. But in looking at the graphic you can see there is a HUGE amount of Reality that I cannot experience with my five senses. There is even an incredible amount of my own reality that I cannot experience with my five senses. This is what the aliens want us to know. There is so much more to reality than we can experience using our five senses.

They explained it in a way that UV waves are passing through us right now, coming from the sun. I can't see them, hear them, taste them, touch them, or feel them but that doesn't make them any less real. And UV waves are only one example, one thing that humans have discovered. The parts of Big Reality that have not yet been discovered by humans are countless.

They told me that when I am asleep, deeply asleep, my personal reality is able to slide over a bit, rotating and opening up my senses to an aspect of Big Reality that is not normally accessible during wakefulness. This is the place where they connect with me. It is my Dream Reality. Around my circle of reality are many other, unknown realities.

Telepathy is one example they use all the time for communication purposes that falls outside those pie-shaped wedges that we call our total reality. Time—the way we experience time—is another, different aspect of the Big Reality. Pretty much anything you can think of that remains a mystery to us can be found in these other parts of reality. We can fly. We can be invisible. But we have to be able to access that whole other chunk of reality. I've had fifty years of experience with these guys and would seriously love to be able to fly. But it's not happening. They are not here to teach these things; they are here to teach us how to find them. And I'm still looking, as much in the dark as anyone else.

They exist in another section of the Reality, the Reality that we are unable to perceive with our five senses, but sometimes we access them in our dreamtime, when our concept of reality is more fluid and free-flowing.

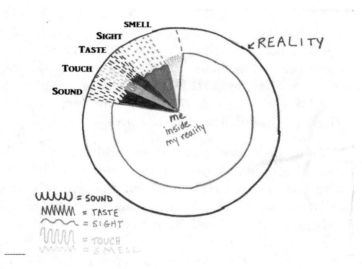

Be open to a greater Reality. You never know what you might find.

\*\*\*

# Chapter 7

# Love

Love is what the aliens are all about. It took me decades to come to this conclusion, but the hints were there all along. *I was told in meditation that I am the Earth's lover. Not in a sexual way, but that I—and many thousands of others—are here to love the Earth. That's all. And that the animals are too.*

*The Middle East corresponds to my heart. Lately my heart has been bothering me. I was told that millions of people are developing heart trouble right now (animals too) in sympathy with Earth because the Middle East is her heart chakra. That's why Jesus came in there. Earth has a broken heart right now. We are each carrying a piece of the pain to relieve the burden on her. So I should bear my pains with pride, as a free will choice I made to help Earth. —September 4, 2002*

A week later I had a dream related to this one; though not specifically about love, it is connected. Note that this was the time period when our relations with Iraq were ramping up in preparation for the "shock and awe" war in 2003.

*Had distinct dream that I was being operated on, that doctors were placing a shield of armor over my chest (specifically my heart) to protect me. My husband was looking over their shoulders. The shield was like a heavy plastic material, royal blue in color, and they were*

116

*screwing it down into my body, into my bones like the clavicle and ribs.*
*—September 10, 2002*

\*\*\*

Back in 1996 I was going through a difficult time emotionally. They encircled me with much unconditional love during that time.

*Love is the true key. There are many false keys; prophecy, money, worship of wrong ideals; there are many wrong keys. LOVE is the right key. LOVE is the only key. Worry and disdain will drive LOVE away. Therefore, replace those thoughts with thoughts of LOVE. There is the expression "love will find a way." That it will. LOVE absolves pain, past and present. LOVE dissolves fear and worry. If LOVE is contained wholly in the heart, there is no room for fear to reside.*

*LOVE does not pay the bills, true, yet neither does worry or fear. And by keeping the heart open to LOVE, the way is made clear for other avenues—new avenues—to come your way. Worry not how, or when. Only LOVE and the rest will take care of itself. —September 11, 1996*

*Dearest beloved, we are here now and always. Live in LOVE. Laugh in LOVE. Enjoy the days of Earth and do not fret. —undated*

*We love you. We are here for a twofold purpose. Teaching and learning, lessons for a lifetime. —1996*

There have been rare occurrences when I have been able to ask a question or two and awakened with the ability to recall the answers. Most of the time I awaken knowing I have been given an enormous amount of information, but it fades away like fine sand that I struggle to grasp between my fingers. Nothing the aliens do is by accident so I'm certain this information is stored somewhere deep in my subconscious mind and hopefully will be accessible when the time is right, when the situation is right. Sometimes, however, they allow me to remember large chunks of material. In the following instance I felt the urge to sit and begin writing, and this is what was put on the paper, not that I "wrote" it per se, but that it came through me in some way and is a message from them. I had been pondering my struggles with finances and wondering why money has always been an issue for me throughout my entire life.

*This is not an individual debt. This is a group karma debt; an extraordinarily large group debt which was incurred long, long ago. It is coming to a head at this time as agreed upon prior to birth into this lifetime. It is a major atonement to your planet Earth.*

*It was a group decision to make this a most difficult time. The struggle will not end until this particular lifetime ends; however that is not necessarily bad. If you knew the wealth you reaped in prior lifetimes, the way money and gold and jewels and power had corrupted in previous lifetimes and added to the great distress now being suffered by your beloved planet, you would have created far greater suffering and struggle for yourself in this lifetime. However, we love you too much to allow further distress.*

*It is also why so many soulmates are coming together at this particular time; for the only thing which truly alleviates the suffering of planet Earth and the souls inhabiting her is unconditional love. It is why your dogs are here. Unconditional LOVE.*

*Do you see how LOVE for one another ties in with your love for your sorrowful planet, your love for the dear voiceless animals, your desire for atonement through struggle? Do you see now how, truly, LOVE is the only answer to each of your questions? —1996*

By 2005 I had developed a better relationship with the aliens and, while I occasionally screamed as a reflex reaction, I was under better control with the communication. That's when they really started with the talks about love.

*Love is multifaceted like a diamond. Yes, you love differently and there is no shame in that—the love for your spouse is obviously different than the love for your children, which is different than the love for your parents, which is different than the love welling in your chest when you observe an awesome sunset, or the love you feel when you worship. But all love comes from a central source. These are all just facets—faces—of the same gem.* [They then showed me a huge, glittering, multifaceted diamond.] ONE SOURCE. ONE DIAMOND. MANY FACETS (FACES). Don't forget to love yourself. —December 9, 2005

* * *

## Messages

I am nobody special. Anyone can receive these messages, anyone can interact with the aliens. I may have had an easier time at the beginning (if you can call those night terrors easy) because I had a pre-birth agreement, but I have been told many times that Earth has reached a very important crossroads, and that all help is needed to assist with enlightenment and a higher spiritual evolution if humankind and Earth are to make it to the next level. If you have a willing heart and mind, if you have the confidence to allow the aliens to "read your heart," then you are invited to interact with them. Reading your heart isn't anything awful. They are forgiving and understanding. I do however try to be a compassionate person, be friendly to everyone I meet, save spiders from the bathroom drain, and have great love and respect for nature and the Earth. I don't harbor ill will to others. I have forgiven those who wronged me in the past, and I have forgiven (and continue to forgive) myself for my own transgressions and ignorance. That is all they are looking for—intent. Genuine intent. Desire for a better world and the desire for you to be a part of creating that new and better world. But you can't fake it or they will know. It must be genuine. At this point it is not a prerequisite that you had any kind of pre-birth contract or any previous contact with them. Heck, you can even have doubts of their very existence; they are more than happy to eliminate that little issue for you. If you hold love in your heart and demonstrate positive intent, I believe they will be looking for you—if you truly desire it and ask them.

I recognize that part of my calling, part of my job with the aliens involves my frequent dreams of leading others to safety, of guiding a large group of people, of talking to soldiers and regular people about the aliens; reassuring others that the aliens are not to be feared. My job is to invite others to join the party, to let people know it's okay! Don't be afraid. You attract what you focus on, so if you focus on aliens being demonic and evil then you may attract some less-than-desirable entities; but if your intentions are pure and you focus on love and harmony, you will be fine. As a precaution, you can do as I do and ask that they come in the pure light and love of the Christ Consciousness, for the best and highest good of all involved.

\*\*\*

## Messages of Hope

In 1996 I was going through some personal crises; acute illness of my daughter and recurring migraine headaches myself. I was worried that a major catastrophe was going to occur at the turn of the millennium on 1/1/2000. Looking back now, I can see that the tone and caliber of the messages completely changed during this time. It was the beginning of the breakdown of my fears. They knew how to use my worries as a means of connecting with me.

These messages are almost angelic in nature. One might come to the conclusion they were delivered by angels, and at the time I did. Years later when I came to meet the alien Ahtehkanah I realized it had been her softly nurturing presence that delivered these messages of hope to me at the time I most needed to hear them.

*Do not worry about time constraints. Yours are not ours. They do not apply to us. Do not force rigid timetables upon yourself. They are not necessary. We will call; or you will call and we will respond when the timing is right so there will be no interruption of our time together, for this is sacred time and you need not feel tense or concerned with naught but this time and the writing. We will connect again soon!!!*

*LOVE LOVE LOVE.* —*August 25, 1996*

*Be of good cheer. Do not cry. Tears bring much sorrow on this plane. In the manner in which you ache to hold your tearful child, dry her eyes and stop her pain, so much multiplied is the desire for us to do the same for you. Remember the great Love your Father has for you; and therefore the love we also have for you.*

*Do not cry, my child. We love you dearly. Do not forget this even in your darkest moment. We hold you in the best way we can; although you cannot feel physical arms around you—we are there, always.* — *August 29, 1996*

*The Earth cries in sorrow. You feel this; it is also your sorrow. This will pass in time. It is working according to plan. Your daughter is one of the special ones, here to elevate the planet. You will be at her side at the necessary time. Do not fear for her safety or for your own.* —*September 29, 1996*

\*\*\*

## Our Creator

*We do not invalidate anyone's faith. It is a testament to the spirit of humanity that anyone has any faith at this time, under the circumstances.* —*undated*

This was the reply I received when I asked about God. I have come to understand over the years, mostly unspoken, that the aliens believe in a Creator unconditionally. It simply is; it's not something to argue about or question, and they are quite confused at humanity's squabbles over it. They accept our Creator as The Source of All rather than limiting Creator to the image of a human sitting on a throne in the clouds.

**East, west, does not matter. All comes from one Source. Time—morning, evening—does not matter. All are one Source.** *—October 7, 2005.* This was in response to my going out at sunrise and noting the western sky aglow with magnificent pinks and purples, yet the sun rises in the east. The reply slipped into my head in Crote's familiar and reassuring male voice.

*They come in the Christ Consciousness, Divine Mind, which is what Jesus embodied during his short life here. Christ consciousness, cosmic consciousness, Divine Mind permeate the universe; it's the unified field that holds everything in its infinite grasp. Love is the glue that holds the universe together. —December 5, 2014*

***

# Notes

## Chapter 1

1. David M. Jacobs, Secret Life: Firsthand Accounts of UFO Abduction (New York: Simon & Schuster, 1992), 43.

2. Andy Bloxam, Aliens Have Deactivated British and US Nuclear Missiles, Say US Military Pilots, September 27, 2010, http://www.telegraph.co.uk.

3. Bob McKeown, Cruel Camera 1982, http://www.youtube.com. Full Documentary.

## Chapter 3

1. Whitley Strieber, Communion: A True Story (New York: Avon Books, 1987).

## Chapter 6

1. Incident Shag Harbour 1967, http://www.richplanet.net.

# About the Author

Donna Lynn was one of those little children who never stopped asking "why?" She studied psychology, world religions, and metaphysics while working in healthcare in the quest for understanding the mind/body/spirit connection.

A wise teacher once told Donna "Your gentleness is your strength." After a lifetime of being told by others that she was too sensitive, Donna decided to embrace her sensitivity when otherworldly beings showed up to answer her question of "why?" She interacted with beings that others couldn't see and visited places that others haven't been, overcoming extreme fear and slowly developing relationships with these entities. She has been advised that now is the time to share these experiences with others and invite them to explore new realms of possibility.

Donna lives in Southern California with a feisty terrier. From the icy waters of the North Atlantic off Nova Scotia, to the warm nurturing Gulf of Mexico with its white sandy beaches, to the vast Pacific Ocean's rhythmic waves and deep mystery, Donna has always felt the call to live near the sea. She enjoys spending time in delightful and imaginative discussion with children, who are still wide-eyed with wonder and open to the endless possibilities of the universe.

# If you liked this book, you might also like:

*The Forgotten Promise*
by Sherry Wilde

*Keepers of the Garden*
by Dolores Cannon

*The Custodians*
by Dolores Cannon

*Children of the Stars*
by Nikki Pattillo

*The Legend of Starcrash*
by Dolores Cannon

For more information about any of the above titles, soon to be released titles, or other items in our catalog, write, phone or visit our website:
Ozark Mountain Publishing, Inc.
PO Box 754, Huntsville, AR 72740
479-738-2348
www.ozarkmt.com

For more information about any of the titles published by Ozark Mountain Publishing, Inc., soon to be released titles, or other items in our catalog, write, phone or visit our website:

Ozark Mountain Publishing, Inc.

PO Box 754

Huntsville, AR 72740

479-738-2348/800-935-0045

www.ozarkmt.com

# Other Books By Ozark Mountain Publishing, Inc.

**Dolores Cannon**
A Soul Remembers Hiroshima
Between Death and Life
Conversations with Nostradamus,
 Volume I, II, III
The Convoluted Universe -Book One,
 Two, Three, Four, Five
The Custodians
Five Lives Remembered
Jesus and the Essenes
Keepers of the Garden
Legacy from the Stars
The Legend of Starcrash
The Search for Hidden Sacred Knowledge
They Walked with Jesus
The Three Waves of Volunteers and the
 New Earth
**Aron Abrahamsen**
Holiday in Heaven
Out of the Archives – Earth Changes
**Justine Alessi & M. E. McMillan**
Rebirth of the Oracle
**Kathryn/Patrick Andries**
Naked In Public
**Kathryn Andries**
The Big Desire
Dream Doctor
Soul Choices: Six Paths to Find Your Life
 Purpose
Soul Choices: Six Paths to Fulfilling
 Relationships
**Patrick Andries**
Owners Manual for the Mind
**Tom Arbino**
You Were Destined to be Together
**Rev. Keith Bender**
The Despiritualized Church
**Dan Bird**
Waking Up in the Spiritual Age
**O.T. Bonnett, M.D./Greg Satre**
Reincarnation: The View from Eternity
What I Learned After Medical School
Why Healing Happens
**Julia Cannon**
Soul Speak – The Language of Your Body
**Ronald Chapman**
Seeing True
**Albert Cheung**
The Emperor's Stargate
**Jack Churchward**
Lifting the Veil on the Lost Continent of Mu
The Stone Tablets of Mu
**Sherri Cortland**
Guide Group Fridays
Raising Our Vibrations for the New Age
Spiritual Tool Box
Windows of Opportunity

**Cinnamon Crow**
Chakra Zodiac Healing Oracle
Teen Oracle
**Michael Dennis**
Morning Coffee with God
God's Many Mansions
**Claire Doyle Beland**
Luck Doesn't Happen by Chance
**Jodi Felice**
The Enchanted Garden
**Max Flindt/Otto Binder**
Mankind: Children of the Stars
**Arun & Sunanda Gandhi**
The Forgotten Woman
**Maiya & Geoff Gray-Cobb**
Angels -The Guardians of Your Destiny
Seeds of the Soul
**Carolyn Greer Daly**
Opening to Fullness of Spirit
**Julia Hanson**
Awakening To Your Creation
**Donald L. Hicks**
The Divinity Factor
**Anita Holmes**
Twidders
**Antoinette Lee Howard**
Journey Through Fear
**Vara Humphreys**
The Science of Knowledge
**Victoria Hunt**
Kiss the Wind
**James H. Kent**
Past Life Memories As A Confederate
 Soldier
**Mandeep Khera**
Why?
**Dorothy Leon**
Is Jehovah An E.T
**Mary Letorney**
Discover The Universe Within You
**Sture Lönnerstrand**
I Have Lived Before
**Donna Lynn**
From Fear to Love
**Irene Lucas**
Thirty Miracles in Thirty Days
**Susan Mack & Natalia Krawetz**
My Teachers Wear Fur Coats
**Patrick McNamara**
Beauty and the Priest
**Maureen McGill**
Baby It's You
**Maureen McGill & Nola Davis**
Live From the Other Side
**Henry Michaelson**
And Jesus Said – A Conversation
**Dennis Milner**
Kosmos

# Other Books By Ozark Mountain Publishing, Inc.

**Guy Needler**
Avoiding Karma
Beyond the Source – Book 1, Book 2
The Anne Dialogues
The History of God
The Origin Speaks
**James Nussbaumer**
The Master of Everything
Mastering Your own Spiritual Freedom
**Sherry O'Brian**
Peaks and Valleys
**Riet Okken**
The Liberating Power of Emotions
**John Panella**
The Gnostic Papers
**Victor Parachin**
Sit a Bit
**Nikki Pattillo**
A Spiritual Evolution
Children of the Stars
**Rev. Grant H. Pealer**
A Funny Thing Happened on the
  Way to Heaven
Worlds Beyond Death
**Karen Peebles**
The Other Side of Suicide
**Victoria Pendragon**
Born Healers
Feng Shui from the Inside, Out
Sleep Magic
**Michael Perlin**
Fantastic Adventures in Metaphysics
**Walter Pullen**
Evolution of the Spirit
**Christine Ramos, RN**
A Journey Into Being
**Debra Rayburn**
Let's Get Natural With Herbs
**Charmian Redwood**
A New Earth Rising
Coming Home to Lemuria
**David Rivinus**
Always Dreaming

**Briceida Ryan**
The Ultimate Dictionary of Dream
  Language
**M. Don Schorn**
Elder Gods of Antiquity
Legacy of the Elder Gods
Gardens of the Elder Gods
Reincarnation...Stepping Stones of Life
**Garnet Schulhauser**
Dance of Heavenly Bliss
Dancing Forever with Spirit
Dancing on a Stamp
**Annie Stillwater Gray**
Education of a Guardian Angel
The Dawn Book
Work of a Guardian Angel
**Blair Styra**
Don't Change the Channel
**Natalie Sudman**
Application of Impossible Things
**L.R. Sumpter**
We Are the Creators
**Dee Wallace/Jarrad Hewett**
The Big E
**Dee Wallace**
Conscious Creation
**James Wawro**
Ask Your Inner Voice
**Janie Wells**
Embracing the Human Journey
Payment for Passage
**Dennis Wheatley/ Maria Wheatley**
The Essential Dowsing Guide
**Jacquelyn Wiersma**
The Zodiac Recipe
**Sherry Wilde**
The Forgotten Promise
**Stuart Wilson & Joanna Prentis**
Atlantis and the New Consciousness
Beyond Limitations
The Essenes -Children of the Light
The Magdalene Version
Power of the Magdalene
**Robert Winterhalter**
The Healing Christ

For more information about any of the above titles, soon to be released titles,
or other items in our catalog, write, phone or visit our website:
PO Box 754, Huntsville, AR 72740
479-738-2348/800-935-0045
www.ozarkmt.com